Tea with God

Everyday Encounters

Paulette Pierce Holloway

WORDS2EMPOWER
PUBLISHERS

Tea With God — Everyday Encounters

Published by: Words2Empower Publishers

1st Printing, 2007

Cover Design: Solomon Edmond
Book Design: Yvonne Vermillion
Book Editor: Chuck Vermillion

ISBN: 978-0-9790213-5-0

For more information, write to:
Paulette Holloway Ministries,
2017 North Capitol Street, NE
Washington, DC 20002

hollowayp@aol.com

OR

Words2Empower Publishers
P.O. Box 4964
Capitol Heights, Maryland, 20791 USA
www.wpublishers.com
1-888-925-BOOK (2665)
For Worldwide Distribution
Printed in Canada

Endorsements

"*Tea With God* gives you a portal to view the intimate relationship between God and a woman who sees God's hand in everything. It propels the reader to seek the same open, intimate and dependent relationship with God. Paulette communicates with God continuously and challenges the readers to do likewise."

- William J Blacquiere President/C.E.O. Bethany Christian Services

"*Tea With God* is a powerful reminder that everyday life is God's Great classroom where He teaches us His lessons of life. Paulette shares her experiences in a manner that will cause the reader to reflect and relate to the message...I found myself smiling, inspired, refreshed and enlightened!"

Dr. Lonise P. Bias, President Certified Family and Teen Life Coach

Table of Contents

ACKNOWLEDGEMENTS 1

CHAPTER I
DOUBLE YOUR MONEY 3

CHAPTER II
BMW 6

Chapter III
LIVING WATER 11

CHAPTER IV
On The Toll Road 14

CHAPTER V
THE WAL-MART RETURN 17

CHAPTER VI
THE EARTHWORM 21

CHAPTER VII
SUDDENLY 23

CHAPTER VIII
ONLY A FLURRY 26

CHAPTER IX
The Champion 29

CHAPTER X
THE SIGNS REFLECT THE LAW 33

CHAPTER XI
GOD CARES ABOUT THE SIMPLE THINGS 37

CHAPTER XII
THE BANANA 40

CHAPTER XIII
THE FIRE IN MY BED. 42

CHAPTER XIV
THE FLOWERS IN KAZAKHSTAN. 45

CHAPTER XV
THE KNOT ON MY SON'S HEAD. 48

CHAPTER XVI
MY DAY IN COURT 50

CHAPTER XVII
THE HAM JUICE. 53

CHAPTER XVIII
FIRE IN THE WASHER. 55

CHAPTER XIX
THE BLOW DRYER. 60

CHAPTER XX 62
KEYS AT THE AIRPORT 62

CHAPTER XXI
MY BIRTHDAY PARTY. 66

CHAPTER XXII
MOVE YOUR CAR 69

CHAPTER XXIII
NO FOOD TO EAT 71

CHAPTER XXV
WHO WOULD HAVE EVER THOUGHT... 75

Acknowledgements

I would like to acknowledge my parents, Charlie Lee (deceased) and Zetta Mae Pierce for their years of encouragement and their wonderful way of preparing me (and my siblings, too) for life. They taught us that we could do anything we set our minds to do; they removed the limits from our thinking. I appreciate those growing-up years in rural Virginia, the great teachers I had in the public schools, and the many family members and friends who helped to raise us.

I would also like to acknowledge my children who have contributed so richly to my life experiences, my siblings who have lived through so much with me, my dear friends who have put up with me over the years, Aglow International who gave me a chance to develop spiritually and to mature as a leader, and my church family who have all nurtured me and helped me to grow. I especially want to acknowledge those close friends who have hounded me to get something written and have not let me give up on my dream to do just that.

If you ever got to know me personally, you would find out that I love the outdoors. I love watching the Majesty of God, The Creator. Put me beside a lake, a stream, or an ocean, and I am lost in THE LORD. Let me watch the birds in flight, the fluffy clouds, or have the rain spray on my face, and I am hopelessly in love with God, with life, and with all that surrounds me. It is no surprise that I get deep revelations and how to make practical applications to my daily life from God's Word, as I find myself in the midst of His Majesty. On the other hand, if I find myself inside, gazing out of a window, just wanting to snuggle in and be reflective, then my other passion, as I meditate on the Goodness of The Lord, is to sip on a mellow cup of tea from a fine china cup. There is just something sweet and peaceful about the gentleness of that touch against my lips. It seems that God comes alive to me, becoming my rest in a weary land or my peace in the time of storm. I find that pulling the curtains on all the hustle and the bustle, shutting out all interruptions, and curling up with a cup of tea seems to bring the Presence of my God within reach. I can hear His Voice; I can think of His Goodness, and I can just meditate on the wonderful God-encounters I may have had recently to remind me of His Glory.

After a further glimpse into my character, you would see that I seem to have a very practical, analytical approach to life. I struggle to understand what appears to me to be illogical thoughts, decisions, and responses. Sometimes, unfortunately, I can be downright impatient with others. Yet, the practical also seems to be a way that God chooses to bring me closer to Him. If I am in the middle of some painful, foolish, or emotional experience, I can count on God to make it much more than that in my life, to make that very experience count. And even then, settling into my reflective and peaceful state is when I seem to better appreciate whatever God is doing in my life.

This collection of encounters has come from my day-to-day walk with God. They are no more special than yours and may sometimes strike you as so ordinary that you wonder why yours are not also written. I am convinced that yours could be, and I pray that this simple work will encourage you to follow that nudge which God may have been pressing on your heart for all these years. I first thought to title the book *Everyday Encounters With God*, a title born out of a message I gave at a "Women's Encounter" at a small church outside of Washington, D.C., a church that has been supportive of me since long before I had acknowledged that I had a call on my life to set the captives free. As things have progressed, this new title, *Tea With God*, just seemed to be a perfect fit. It speaks of who I am and how God has chosen to fashion me. I pray that you enjoy reading the encounters as much as I have enjoyed reliving them while putting them to pen. I also pray that you will be encouraged to find a simple, quiet "tea-time" for yourself, so that you, too, can sweetly commune with God.

CHAPTER I

Double Your Money

"And he said, A certain man had two sons. The younger of them said to his father, Father, give me my portion of goods that falleth to me. And he divided unto them his living. AND not many days after the younger son gathered all together, and took his journey into a far country, and there wasted his substance with riotous living. And when he had spent all, there arose a mighty famine in the land; and he began to be in want."

Luke 15:11-14 KJV

I had the privilege of raising eight children at different intervals in their lives, and some of them stayed in my care longer than others. I have one daughter who came to live with me when she was two years old and is just two months younger than my youngest son. She grew up with my son almost as his twin.

Though very close in age, these two children were, and still are, as different as night and day. There is not one thing I can think of that I can say they did alike. My son is a very deep thinker, serious and always more mature than his years. My daughter, on the other hand, is quite a free spirit, uninhibited, generous even with her necessary possessions, and seemingly unconcerned about tomorrow.

There came a time, when they were around ten years old, that a school carnival was scheduled to be in the neighborhood. The carnival was set for a Friday, and on the Sunday before, a generous family member gave each of the children $5. They both remembered the upcoming carnival and decided to ask me to keep their money until the day it would be needed. I thought this was a good idea, so I decided to give them a little motivation to save the entire amount. I took the money and explained that I would be willing to double any amount up to their entire $5 on Friday at carnival time. They both thought it was a great deal and vowed not to spend any money during the week.

Each day of the week, however, Lea came to me and asked for some portion of her money. Each time she asked, I resisted, reminding her of how much she could gain if she was patient for just a few days. Each time, however, she insisted on just one dollar, explaining that she still had several dollars to be doubled. On Friday morning, it was time to go to school for the carnival and time for me to give the children their share of the money. I had deliberately gotten my ten dollars ready (one five and five singles) and spread them out on the bed. I then called the children in and took their money from its place. I asked Bryan how much he had, and he proudly announced, "Five dollars." I asked how much more I should give him, and he immediately rattled out, "Five dollars." I gave him his money, and he went joyously on his way.

I turned to Lea and went through the same ritual. She sadly said she only had $1, but then she began to negotiate for more of my dollars. I would not make any such deals, and finally, while looking very sad, she took her $2 and began to leave. I wanted her to understand what had just happened, so I called her back to explain why I could not give her more. I explained that each day that she made the decision to spend some of her money, she was also making a decision to reduce the blessings she had coming to her at the end of the week. I explained that every time I tried to stop her from making an unwise decision because I already knew of the consequence, she insisted on abandoning my counsel and living for the pleasure of that moment. She'd had her fun all week, spending and enjoying her money, but it was impossible for her to enjoy the moment of pleasure and the blessing that comes with waiting with patience for the promise.

Lea left and went to the carnival, and I sat on the floor and cried. I wanted so much to give her as much money as her brother had gotten, yet I knew that it would not have been fair to do so. I sat there, weeping, as the Spirit of The Lord spoke to my heart and reminded me of how many times I had behaved as Lea had. How many times had He wanted to doubly bless me, had He nudged me to wait patiently for His best, had He watched with his heart aching for me because He had known the outcome? And how many times had I indulged in the pleasures for a season and robbed myself of the full treasure in the end? I think of that hard lesson, even now, and ask The Lord to help me, to strengthen me, to keep me, so that I don't miss out on all the wonderful blessings he has designated just for me, and that I don't mess around and double some pitiful (lesser) amount that cannot be compared to what would have been mine if I had waited on God.

CHAPTER II

ℬℳ𝒲

"But God hath chosen the foolish things of the world to confound the wise; and God hath chosen the weak things of the world to confound the things which are mighty."
I Corinthians 1:27 KJV
"Who then is Paul, and who is Apollos, but ministers by whom ye believed, even as the Lord gave to every man? I have planted, Apollos watered; but God gave the increase."
I Corinthians 3:5-6 KJV

As you get to know me, you quickly discover that I like new cars. It is not that I buy cars that I do not like, it is simply that I have no loyalty to cars I have driven for a while, so I trade them often. It was late spring of 1994, and I had been working my way toward a new car for a few months. I had a very fine and well-operating 1992 Volvo station wagon (my fourth in ten years), but I began the road to its demise by letting my eye and my conversation wander toward newer models.

I had been eyeing the BMWs for a while and decided that along with some other major life changes I was experiencing, I should have a new car and a new attitude. I did my BMW homework (short of the pricing) and got excited about all the features and the differences in what the model numbers meant. I went to the BMW dealer and looked at the new cars.

I did not have the money to invest in what I wanted, because they were much pricier than I had expected. Determined, though, to see this plan through, and after walking around the lot until nearly closing, I decided on a black 318i (I really don't like black cars; my favorite is gold.) with no particularly exciting features. I formulated more of my plan as I walked back to the showroom.

I went to the salesman, who in my opinion had not been very helpful, and began to negotiate a deal.

We were in a debate over what I would pay, and it seemed as though I was not winning. I am a stubborn negotiator, and this tall, young man did not know that he was no match for me. He insisted that I had to go in a certain direction, but I was not willing to consider his recommendation. I decided that this obviously was not the car for me, or at least not the dealership for me, so I shifted gears. I told the salesman that it was too bad for him that we could not agree. I told him to have a great day and stood as if to leave. He was grossly disappointed and began to try again.

While standing up, I noticed a beautiful, gold 325i in the showroom that I somehow had not spied before. It drew me like a magnet, and I gravitated toward it in the middle of the young man's new pitch. It had EVERYTHING that I could ever imagine and some things that I couldn't (My son tells me that I really like gadgets.). I got this quickening in my heart and began to listen for a word from God. I cannot honestly say that I heard a word from God, but I surely can say that my heart was racing in a most excited way. I turned abruptly and went back to the salesman. I told him that the car on the showroom floor, with that wonderful on-board computer, was mine. The sunroof, power locks, power windows, power seats, and full-size spare tire had completely won my heart. He chuckled in a very polite way, because this car was a few thousand dollars more than the one whose price I was negotiating, which clearly indicated that I could not afford it.

I emphatically informed him that I was not leaving without that car, that I did not care about how it cost more than the other one, or that it was only thirty minutes from closing time, "Do whatever it takes to put me in this car today!" He was quite taken by my attitude, and I began to make all manner of faith statements (which I am not really prone to do in that "name it and claim it" kind of way). My statements went from sounding like "faith personified" to down-right arrogant. They sounded like, "This car was made for me! I had to come to this dealership, today, for my car. There is an unadvertised special associated with this particular car that you may not know about."

He seemed totally perplexed by my behavior; then, out of his mouth came the most inappropriate statement imaginable, "You remind me of someone who speaks in tongues." Now, what a comment! He went on to say (as I stood there with my mouth wide open) that some girl he knew had just been talking to him about people who speak in tongues and "all that weird stuff", and, somehow, the way I was acting made him think of that girl and their conversation. Then, just as inappropriately, he wanted to know if I knew anything about that kind of thing.

I asked if it would make any difference in the closing of my deal if I was able to give him any insight. He wasn't so sure about that, but he certainly was interested if I knew anything that could help him. But before I was able to respond to his "speaking in tongues" question, he remembered that there was a special rebate on the BMW on the showroom floor that was exclusively designated for that car (Honestly, I promise you he did.). He started clicking away on his calculator and jotting down figures, actually seeming excited about what he had remembered.

Since he didn't really answer me the way I had expected and genuinely wanted an answer to his question, I perceived (I'm a little slow sometimes.) that a plan had to be unfolding. I knew God well enough to know that a door had been opened, so I sized up the young man, decided he was the one who needed help, and decided to help him out voluntarily (before I got a lightening bolt). I dismissed my plans of buying a car and went about the business of the Kingdom.

I asked him if he knew anything about salvation and what that meant. He knew a little but didn't really understand much. So I asked him if he knew a lot about BMWs. Of course he knew about BMWs; after all, he was a BMW salesman. So what proceeded out of my mouth was the plan of salvation and abundant life, BMW style. It sounded like this: "Salvation is the guarantee that when you die, you get to live again forever in Heaven with Jesus. Jesus is the Son of God whom God sent to the Earth to die for all mankind, to die for our sins, to give us a way to get back to God who made us and wants us to be with him forever. Salvation is basic; it gets you to Heaven. It affords you all the rights and privileges of any other child of God who has followed the basic plan. A BMW 318i is basic. It gets you into the BMW family. It is a good car that affords its owner all the rights and privileges of any BMW owner. You are a proud BMW owner, and no one can say that you do not have a BMW. So salvation is like having a BMW 318i. It's the basic guarantee that you are in the family."

He was definitely hooked by this point, so I continued, "Now, if you were offered a free BMW, any kind you wanted, and you had a choice of the least to the greatest, would you prefer a BMW 318i, or would you prefer a larger and more prestigious model like the 740i? The BMW 740i has more power, more features, more prestige, more everything. You drive with a different level of confidence when you're in that 740i."

He quickly interrupted me with his response that he would prefer the 740i.

"Well," I explained, "speaking in tongues is like that 740i. Not only do you have salvation, which guarantees you eternal life, but you also have the power to live an abundant life right here on Earth while you're waiting to go to Heaven. You have the power to love more, to live holy, to lead others to Jesus, and to just have joy in the midst of any trials. Speaking in tongues is only one

9

small piece of evidence that you are walking in the power of the Holy Spirit. You never have to speak in tongues to get to Heaven, but it surely is nice to have the power for abundant living before you get there. So what would you rather have, a 325i or a 740i if you had to drive a car?"

He admitted that a 740i made more sense, if the choice was yours to make. The moment ended, and I did not say another word about Kingdom things. Miraculously, the negotiations started moving in my favor, and in less than one hour, I drove my new BMW off the lot. It was an exciting and joyous experience.

I never saw that young man again, though I went looking for him a few times. He had moved on to another job, I was told. I have no idea where he may be today, but I believe in my heart of hearts that I will see that young man in eternity! I believe that God had set him up to have the seed planted by his friend, and then He had sent me along to water the seed, just so He could get the increase. My prayer is that I never miss the opportunities which God orchestrates to win souls to the Kingdom, and which might even include a reward in the plan for my obedience.

Chapter III
Living Water

*"Jesus answered and said unto her, 'Whosoever drinketh
of this water shall thirst again: But whosoever drinketh of the
water that I shall give him shall never thirst; but the water
that I shall give him shall be in him a well of water springing
up into everlasting life.' "*

John 4:13, 14 KJV

A few years ago, I had the privilege of serving as the weekend
speaker for a women's retreat. It was held up in the mountains on
an old and quaint estate which had been transformed into a bed
& breakfast and a secluded retreat spot. The large, old house was
tucked away on a wooded mountainside, with trees, streams, and
wild flowers. The trees were so thick that sunshine struggled to
break through to the ground, and despite the warming springtime
air, left-over snow still made its presence known in a few spots. It
was my kind of place. It was the kind of place that I could often
get lost in and not be concerned about becoming lost.

I was between sessions on this Saturday afternoon, and I
decided to take a walk to check out the beautiful scenery. I wandered
for a while, pushing back brush, stepping over water spots, and
listening to the sound of birds chatting in the trees. I stepped into
a clearing of about ten feet wide and stumbled upon a shallow
stream. The sound of the flowing water caught my attention
before I actually saw the water glistening in the stingy sunlight.
The treetops had formed a perfect arch over the stream, and the
squirrels and birds kept in constant motion in the branches.

As I approached the stream, I bent to study my find. It was
pretty shallow, maybe six inches or so. It was moving quickly and
provided protection for the rocks near its surface. There were

11

several rocks of varying degrees of brown that looked friendly enough to support my body weight, so I took off my shoes and stepped onto the rocks. The water was quite cool, but not cool enough to discourage me.

I then decided to have fun playing in the water. I picked up a twig that was half buried in the mud, and I began to stir around in the water. I was just close enough to the stream that each time I dug my intruding twig into the streambed, the water would become muddied. I became fascinated with this, so I did the same thing over and over. What amazed me about that little activity was that each time I muddied the water, in an instant, it was clear and clean again. Muddy — clean. Muddy — clean. No matter how deep I dug into the streambed, the fast-flowing movement of the water would wash away the mud in an instant.

I stepped off the rocks and stood there on the edge of the stream fighting back the tears. I was overwhelmed by the Presence of The Lord. His spirit was speaking to my heart, saying that His Blood was like that flowing stream. Each time I commit a sin and muddy the waters, His blood rushes along and washes that sin away. No matter how deeply I might muddy the waters, the rushing power of His Blood is so great, so swift, that one simple confession keeps the stream flowing, washing away even the worst of my mess. The thought of God's Incredible Goodness and Mercy settled into my heart and led me to a place of peace beyond my imagination.

I moved from that precious spot near the stream, as I became able, and I soon stumbled upon an old, deserted gazebo, which looked as if it had been lost in the midst of the woods. It was clad in faded and chipping paint, and, as I approached, there was an unusual smell associated with it. I stepped onto its outer ledge, and as I peaked inside, I saw a puddle of water trapped in one corner, a few dead leaves, and some rich green moss. The water was obviously stale, having been trapped there for a while. There was the smell of vegetation rotting and just an all-around unclean feel about the place.

I stood there for a few seconds, considering what I saw and smelled, and, again, I was overwhelmed by the Presence of The Lord. My heart was sensing the contrast between the ever-flowing stream I had previously encountered and this stagnant and smelly water trapped in the base of this gazebo. The stagnant water was like our souls before we accept Jesus Christ as our Lord and Savior, dead, with no hope of being changed into something more vibrant, and doomed to a smelly, rotten end. The stream, on the other hand, represented life, hope, joy, and freedom — our souls after we accept Christ. The contrast was so great; the thought of eternal death was so devastating, that I could not help but think of the Father's Heart, as He looked upon us, longing for us to choose the flowing stream, but seeing us often choosing the stagnant water instead.

CHAPTER IV

On The Toll Road

*"And it shall come to pass that before they call, I will
answer; and while they are yet speaking, I will hear."*
Isaiah 65:24 KJV

I have developed some very unwise habits over the years, and
one of them is traveling alone for long distances without stopping to
get traveling cash. Sometimes, when it seems inconvenient, when I
don't feel like stopping, or I'm under the time-gun, I simply choose
not to stop. I tell myself that I will have plenty of opportunities to
get cash or that I really have no need for cash, because, after all, I
have my ATM card. My car is properly serviced, is full of gas, and
has no reason to malfunction on the highway. So, as foolish as this
sounds, my intelligence escapes me, and off I go.

The December when one of my life-long friends turned fifty, I
had the privilege of celebrating with her at her home in New Jersey.
I was living in Washington, D.C. at the time, so I made plans to make
the four-hour drive on a Saturday afternoon, since the party was
planned for early evening. We had already decided that I would
spend the night so that I would not grow too weary on the highway
alone, late at night. I had a mid-morning commitment that ended
later than I had anticipated, so as usual, I left under the time-gun.
I checked my purse and I had less than $15.00, but that was okay
because the car was ready for travel. I tried to calculate in my mind
the tolls along the way, decided I had enough cash, and set out.

On my way to New Jersey, I used about half my cash for the tolls.
When I arrived in New Jersey, as I approached the neighborhood
where my friend lived, I noticed a bank, my bank, nestled just off the
main street. The bright green letters seemed almost as if they were
flashing at me. I got an instant nudge in my spirit that I should go to

that bank and withdraw some cash, but I quickly shrugged off the warning and stayed on course. I told myself that I had plenty of time on my way out of town to visit the ATM drive-through, so there was no reason to make arrival even later by interrupting my travel.

I had a wonderful time seeing old friends and family at the birthday party, and we stayed up much too late while having fun. After about two hours of sleep, we made our way to early service, took communion, and returned home for breakfast. (Now, you would think that after all the time in church, taking communion and all, that I would really have been in a more spiritual mind, hearing Him, the Holy Spirit, speak more clearly.) My good friend had planned to give me some clothes that were closer to my size than hers, so as I prepared to go, she piled five nice blazers into my arms. The colors were great, and there were some for summer and some for winter. What a treat! After a few hugs and kisses, I grabbed my loot and got under way for my return trip.

In just a few minutes of travel, I was back in that same neighborhood where I had seen the bank as I had arrived. I saw the big green sign announcing my stop. I got the same Holy Spirit nudge. Instead of stopping, however, I counted my money in my head, made my usual dumb decision, and proceeded onto the highway.

Once on the highway, I began singing and praising and looking forward to my return home. I paid the toll on the New Jersey Turnpike. I paid the toll at the Delaware Bridge. I started thinking that there had been no sister toll going north to match this toll, but I must have been wrong. Oh, well. I approached a toll entering Maryland that proudly announced that I needed two dollars. That was impossible, because I should only need $1.00 for the Baltimore Tunnel! What was this toll, and where did it come from?

With my palms sweaty, I pulled over to the shoulder and began counting my money. I had $1.58. I turned my purse upside down. I shook it. I pulled it apart — nothing. I looked at the cars speeding by and dismissed the thought to get out and ask someone for a dollar. I then noticed another lady in a car just beyond the toll booth, writing something under the scrutiny of a toll official. *Wow, she must be signing a pledge,* I thought. *Maybe I should try that. No, there's got to be 42 cents in my car somewhere.* I began looking under the seats. *Oh, thank You, Lord, one dime, one nickel, and two pennies. Now all I need, Lord, is one little-bitty quarter, Lord. Please????* I pulled the mats out, nothing. I moved the seats, nothing. I worked up a real sweat, nothing. Okay, it was decision time. Should I go plead my case to the toll attendant, begging for a 25 cent break or just ask to sign the pledge? As I humbled myself and gave up, I started putting my car back together. I put the seats back and threw the blazers that I had tossed to the floor in haste back on the seat.

I wonder… No… not likely. Well, what could it hurt? I desperately started going through each jacket pocket from the loot given me by my friend. As I put my hand into the last pocket, feeling totally defeated because all the other pockets had been empty, I felt it — one quarter!!! Can you believe it? I had pulled together $2.00! *Oh, Lord, you are too good to me!*

I paid my toll with a handful of coins and with tears streaming down my face. I rejoiced for several miles. I kept thinking about how unfaithful I was and how faithful God is. Even when He has done all that is necessary to help me but I choose to ignore His help, He continues to be faithful, to see about me, and to provide for me.

I quickly realized that I had another toll to go, so, at the next opportunity, I took the exit for a service area. In seconds, I spotted an ATM machine inside the facility and I withdrew some cash. I returned to my trip, still somewhat misty-eyed and grateful, and I proceeded toward my destination. I meditated on the goodness of The Lord for quite some time, before finally succumbing to a heavy sigh of relief that God loves me so much that He prepares answers for me even before I call with the questions. But then, He said He would.

CHAPTER V

The Wal-mart Return

"Charity suffereth long, and is kind; charity envieth not; charity vaunteth not itself, is not puffed up, Doth not behave itself unseemly, seeketh not her own, is not easily provoked, thinketh no evil;"

I Corinthians 13:4,5 KJV

My grandson lives with his mom in another state, and I don't get to see him as often as I'd like. We have managed to develop a wonderful relationship despite the distance between us, so I look for any opportunity to get together with him. He was approaching his eighth birthday, and I wanted to do something special for him. His birthday comes in May and in the middle of the school calendar, so I decided to bless him with a little birthday party at school. He lives 2 hours away, so I contacted his teacher and his mother to make sure my plan was welcomed. His birthday was falling on a Friday, so I decided to take the day off, make the two-hour trip, and then return home after the party.

Two nights before the party, I received a call from his mother who was quite upset. It seemed that my grandson had done something that had distressed his mother, and she was going to punish him for his act. She was calling me to say that she was not going to give him the cake for his birthday that she had planned to take to school the day before his birthday. She finally calmed down and decided to proceed with her original plan.

As soon as she was off the phone, I began to vent my anger. Why would she decide to take a cake to the school on the day before his birthday, knowing that we had agreed that I would come the following day, on his birthday? Why couldn't she just let me have that one special thing? She knew that he had never had a

17

party at school before! Why couldn't the party she gave him wait until next year? The questions went on like that for a while, as I made myself angrier by the minute. Well, I would fix her; I would give this child a great party.

What you need to know here is that the teacher had given me specific instructions about what I could do. The party could only be given during lunchtime and only in the cafeteria. There would only be 30 minutes for both lunch and the party. There were 16 children in the class, and they would be leaving the cafeteria to proceed to another class, or, in other words, they do NOT need to cart around extra junk.

I left home nearly empty-handed and made a decision to stop at the Wal-Mart closest to my grandson's school and shop for ice cream, cupcakes, fruit drinks, and anything else that caught my eye. This trip was coming at a time when I did not have a high volume of finances (son in college, single parent, etc.) and I was on a very tight budget, but I had a plan in mind of what I wanted to purchase.

Once in the Wal-Mart, I began the execution of my plan. As I approached sections of the store, things began to draw me. I bought fancy birthday plates and hats and favors and much-too-much stuff. I bought cards and two gifts and extra items. I had enough ice cream, cupcakes, and little juice boxes for 20 people because of the way some of the items were packaged. I had hoped to get individual cups of ice cream that came packaged with their own spoon, but I did not find that, so I ran back to get spoons. When I reached the register, I had spent over $40.00 for this simple, less than 30 minute long birthday party for 8 year olds. Mild feelings of poor wisdom crept into my emotional view, but I certainly knew what to do with them. They could not find a home in me; after all, this was for my grandson!

18

I made it to the school just before the teacher was about to give up on me. I had bags full of goodies. Lunch was nearly over and we hustled to get things set up quickly. I heard about the cake from the day before as I was preparing. The children were excited to have two parties in two days, and my grandson was the man of the hour. As I was being rushed by the teacher, I failed to pull out half of what was in my six bags. We didn't need the spoons; the cafeteria had those. There was no time for hats or favors and no need for plates and cups; we just used the tray that held the children's food. Only ten children were in class, so there was no need to open the second package of ice cream, cupcakes, or juice. There was no need for napkins; they were already there. We ate and sang and took some pictures in less than 15 minutes. My grandson left the party with a bag of two gifts, two cards, and a lot of smiles. I left the party with four bags, wet kisses on my face, and a slightly foolish heart.

What in the world (or out of the world, for that matter) was I going to do with all that stuff, especially partly-melted ice cream? Well, I was going to take it all back to Wal-Mart, make up some cock-a-mamie story, and throw myself on the mercy of the 'Customer Service Court'. So I went back to Wal-Mart. I was trying to think of a good story, but nothing would come to me. I took all my bags in with me and proceeded, quite timidly, to the customer-service counter. There was a little old lady in front of me that took what seemed like an eternity to be helped.

Okay, now it was my turn. I simply put the bags on the counter, showed my receipt, and explained that I had made the purchases less than one hour earlier for a party, but only half the children had been in class, "Can I *PLEASE* return some of the items?"

I announced the fact that I had ice cream and cupcakes (which I simply knew I could not return), and the sweet, young lady said, "Oh, not a problem, but I would appreciate it if you would place the ice cream in that refrigerator right at the end of the counter."

19

I did, and she counted out my refund, gave me a smile, and sent me on my way — $20 richer!

Before I could reach the exit door, the Holy Spirit was already doing His Work. I immediately received a deep sense of God speaking to my heart, *"Even though your motives were not honorable, your decisions were not wise, and your outcome was not profitable, I still love you and I have chosen to bless you. You can do nothing about My choice to bless you except receive it or reject it. Which do you choose? You must know that I am The God who loves you even when you are not perfect; rather, I love you because you are not perfect. I choose to bless you because of your pure desire to bless your grandson. You did that, and now I do this. I love you."*

There are no words that can describe the depth of love I felt in those few moments, and I believe that my heart was changed forever. I was totally overwhelmed by my own impure heart and by the unconditional love that God had chosen to pour out on me. I realized that I never have to be in competition with my grandson's mother or anyone else. I never need to measure my worth by how much I am able to do for others. I need only to walk out I Corinthians 13 in the purest way I know and believe that my walk will bless those lives around me and will bless God my Father, too.

CHAPTER VI
The Earthworm

"Thou wilt keep him in perfect peace, whose mind is stayed on thee: because he trusteth in thee."
Isaiah 26:3 KJV

I was sitting on the front-porch steps of our home at around six o'clock one mid-July morning, as I had so many other times while spending some time with THE LORD. The steps were surrounded by much-too-large shrubbery on either side, making a sort of green haven for me as I peered up at the beautiful sky. As I sat there on this particular morning, I was burdened with the cares of life, and I wanted to fix all that was troubling me. There was something I felt that I needed to do to make the situation in my home better. My marriage and family were in trouble, and my husband seemed to be totally oblivious to the problem. The family seemed no longer to be a priority, and the children were asking questions. I was constantly crying out for help from THE LORD, from other people, and from anyone who would listen. Well, this morning was THE LORD's turn again, so I began my usual preoccupation with my situation.

As I began weeping and rocking, my tear-filled eyes caught a glimpse of an earthworm wiggling its way toward my foot. (Fortunately, I think worms are cute!) I leaned forward to look more closely, and as I wiped my eyes, I noticed two very-small green leaves, two of many that had fallen from the shrubs. They were stuck to the beginning and the end of my slimy, little friend as he wiggled along. I was immediately overtaken by compassion and decided that I needed to help this poor worm to be freed of its "baggage". My thought was to pluck the leaves off with a little twig that I had picked up from the ground, so I patiently and quietly watched this wiggly creature, while looking for my chance to help (rescue) him. For what seemed like an eternity, the worm wiggled along the cemented walkway in front of my foot, dragging the leaves along. Oh, they looked ever so burdensome. Watching the worm while unconsciously handling the twig, being slightly intrigued by its miniature tree-form, and reflecting on God, I then became distracted by the beautiful sky peaking just over the top of my neighbor's house. I may have been lost in God's splendor for a few minutes, because I lost my focus on the earthworm's "situation" for just a little while. Ultimately, the movement of the worm caught my attention once again, and I was totally in awe of what I saw. Both the leaves had worked themselves off the worm, apparently by the natural motion of its own body as it was making its way to its next destination. The same natural motion that caused the collection of the "baggage" was the very thing that caused the worm's liberation.

I was speechless! I immediately got the sense that the Spirit of The Lord was saying to me that my "baggage", too, could fall away in the same progressive manner, if I changed my focus from *it* to *Him*. I first must realize that the "baggage" will come along with the life I have chosen to live for Christ. Secondly, I must realize that if I take my eyes off the situations of life just long enough to realize God's Presence, He will keep me in perfect peace and relieve the burdens, too. I may never be able to change the situation or the person, but I can certainly allow THE LORD to change me in the midst of it all. The lesson was well learned and tucked away for future use, and I sensed a smile in God's heart, knowing that I had come just a little closer to where He wants me to be — the place of PERFECT PEACE.

CHAPTER VII

Suddenly

"And Hezekiah rejoiced, and all the people, that God has prepared the people: for the thing was done suddenly."

II Chronicles 29:36 KJV

I was sitting on a rocky bank on an obscure corner of the shoreline of the Chesapeake Bay, stealing a moment from my fellow retreat-goers. The morning was misty, and the sun was just beginning to make its impression on the distant ripples in the water. There were three or four sailboats intermittently dispersed throughout the bay, seemingly drifting just for the fun of it. I watched a few gulls fly overhead while they scouted the surface of the water for food. I sat, studying the mist and thinking about the elementary school science that still proudly intruded into my thoughts with the definition of a cloud (a mass of condensed water vapor floating around in the atmosphere) and then of fog (a low cloud touching the Earth). I decided the mist was too thin and light to be fog, and I moved on to pretending that the shapes made in the distance were people on those sailboats stepping out into their morning to enjoy the water. It had been a busy retreat weekend for me thus far. I was serving as a prayer counselor, and there were several first-timers who really needed to be disciplined. I had devoted a great deal of THE LORD's time to simply being available, and I had not been left unemployed.

This morning, though, I thought I wanted some quiet time, as I was really hungry for a word from THE LORD. I cannot say how long I sat on the rocks, making up stories, defining shapes in the distance, sometimes paying attention to the scenes of nature right around me, and sometimes getting lost in my thoughts. As I sat, my thoughts had become noticeably dominant and had begun to remind me of some things going on in my life that I

23

would like to have seen already come to pass. There were things that I believed were challenging my walk and my witness, things that I had begun to hate. The state of my marriage was my favorite theme, because it was so totally unreflective of my heart toward a good and godly marriage. How was I able to pray for everyone else's situation and not see God do something with the crazy way my own family was living? What was wrong with my faith? Why was I not demanding that the enemy take his hands off my situation? These were the same thoughts that had betrayed me many times before; just when I would think that I had overcome, they would start cheating and breaking the rules by invading precious time I had been able to carve away to be in His Presence. I began fighting this preoccupation with my thoughts and knew I was being beaten badly. "How long?" I cried out in desperation.

There was no answer, and being determined not to waste this precious time, I began again to focus on the sailboats in the distance and imagine what it must have been like for Peter to walk on the water. As I was losing myself in that intriguing thought, out of nowhere there began a roar, seemingly under my feet. It was a roar much like an old truck engine, and it became stronger and stronger as I sat there. Then, suddenly, a fountain of water surged right up in front of me, as if propelled by the preceding roar. The water shot up into the air near my feet, with the roaring sound escalating, and then immediately subsiding. Gone! No noise! No fountain! Not even a low tide! Nothing! And the spirit of THE LORD whispered in my heart, *"Suddenly!"*

It was startling to say the least, and I pondered in my heart (like Mary in the Book of Luke) what could have happened. I did not have much time to ponder, because in another instant, the roaring noise started again and the fountain of water gushed upward, this time a little closer, making a splash onto my feet. Then, again, I heard that soft breathy sound, *"Suddenly."*

24

It was such a powerful experience, because the shoreline was a complete contrast to this personal gusher I was getting. There was not even a noticeable ebb and flow of the tide washing against the rocks. That water was perfectly calm!

Somehow, in my heart, I knew God was giving me a word of hope. The volumes of dialogue that flooded my heart after that single, simple word, "Suddenly", made me certain that God had spoken life into my spirit, so much so that I am amazed even in writing this account of its lasting effect on me. Somehow, I knew that THE LORD wanted me to be encouraged and to hold on to HIM, no matter what. He wanted me to rest in HIM, to trust HIM to take care of not just me, but all the things going on around me. He knew my heart's desire, and He would handle those desires in His Own Way and in His Own Time. The answers would come so suddenly that just like that gusher, I would know beyond any doubt that it was Him.

I was "suddenly" energized. I had a new hope. I knew that He could take care of even my reputation (ha, ha — like I really had one outside of HIM) that might appear compromised by all the "things" going on in my life. I believed that THE LORD would use those "things" to bring HIMSELF glory, despite anything I could see. I also believe that He does the same thing today in each of our lives. I believe that if we love Him, He works all those "things" together for good. I encourage you to listen for your own roar, your own fountain, or for whatever He chooses to use to get your attention and to reassure your spirit. He is right in the middle of those "things" in your life, and the change that He effects on your behalf will come "Suddenly!"

CHAPTER VIII

Only A Flurry

*"And when the servant of the man of God was risen early,
and gone forth, behold, a host compassed the city both with
horses and chariots. And the servant said unto him, 'Alas, my
master! How shall we do?' And he answered him,'Fear not:
for they that be with us are more than they that be with them.'
And Elisha prayed, and said, 'Lord, I pray thee, open his eyes
that he may see. AND the Lord opened the eyes of the young
man; and he saw: and, behold, the mountain was full of horses
and chariots of fire round about Elisha.' "*

II Kings 6:15-17 KJV

It was my first-born son's 30th birthday. He had been a near-Christmas baby, foreordaining me to be in the hospital three days before Christmas. I was alone again this year on his birthday, because he was incarcerated yet another year. I was spending my last day of winter vacation in the mountains of Western Virginia and trying to make the best of those last, quiet moments before THE LORD. I got up, wrapped in my soft blanket, and pulled the cushiony, upholstered chair to my favorite spot, right in front of the balcony door, my designated prayer closet. I opened the drapes and deeply drank in the snow-covered scenery. High up on the mountain, the private chalets peeped out through the trees. The golf course directly in front of my window was covered with snow. The furniture on my balcony had the unmelted snow of the days gone by. I inhaled deeply, then exhaled very exaggeratedly a few times.

Somewhat hesitantly, I dropped into the chair, remembering that it was my last morning but yet expectantly moving into the presence of THE LORD. I had begun to softly thank and praise God, beginning to drift into His Presence, and I noticed some

26

seemingly faint mist in the space outside the window that I was sure had not been there when I'd first looked out over the beautiful landscape. In just a few seconds of pondering whether I was imagining the mist, it became more prominent and erased any doubts of its reality. It was a bit unbelievable, in that the sky was a perfect blue with white, fluffy clouds just at the peak of the mountain across the golf course, yet directly in front of my window, the sky was dull and gray. I leaned back and closed my eyes, as I thought on the goodness of THE LORD and how awesome He is to be able to have such concurrent contrasts in nature. I opened my eyes after what had to be only seconds, and a good bit of snow was falling outside the balcony. I chuckled aloud at the contrast of the blue sky and the thickening snow.

In less than two minutes (suddenly), the snow was thick and threatening. I was now watching a serious-looking snowstorm. I continued to sit in the presence of THE LORD and worship Him as I watched the snow. It got heavier and heavier. I was taken in by the beauty of the falling snow, and I drifted deeper into worship. I shifted my gaze to the blue sky just above the snow clouds and marveled at God. Sitting there, my thoughts began to drift, reminding me that my check-out time was less than two hours away and that my drive home would take yet another two hours. Did I dare become anxious about all the snow swirling in front of me?

My thoughts traveled along the narrow, winding road leading back out to the main highway, a road I knew to be treacherous even in good weather. I thought more about whether to panic, as I watched the snow, then I had my thoughts answered by the view of the beautiful, blue sky just above the storm. I kept watching the blue sky, and slowly the snow started lessening. I totally lost sight of the snow, as I intently watched the blue sky and the white, fluffy clouds that had begun to drift toward me. In a few minutes, the fluffy clouds were just overhead and had pushed the snow

27

and the gray sky right out of view. All that thick, heavy snowfall had traveled to where I was, had traveled over me, and had kept on traveling. All I did was focus on the blue sky.

In another few seconds, the newborn sun broke through with splendor, and all that was left of the snowstorm was an incidental flake floating past.

Deep in my heart, I sensed that THE LORD was saying to me that even when the thick of the storm was in my face, what I saw was not as it appeared. I believe that He wanted me to recognize that I keep watching the wrong view. I need to look more closely for the blue sky beyond the storm. Surely I can check out the contrast; I will often be able to marvel at His Greatness in doing so. But I really need to grasp that the storm is temporary. The real scene is the constant, blue sky above the storm. The real scene is highlighted by the fluffy, white clouds that are moving toward me, forcing the gray sky into retirement. All I really need to do is stand still and let the storm pass. I need not be thrown or shaken by what I see. It's only temporary. It has no lasting effect. It's only a flurry!

CHAPTER IX

The Champion

"...and that all this assembly may know that the Lord saves not with sword and spear; for the battle is the Lord's and he will give you into our hand."

I Samuel 17:47 KJV

The account of this day warms my heart as I remember it. It was mid-January, and I was at a new time-share resort enjoying some much needed rest, escaping from the cares of this world. It had been a sweet day of reading, meditation, listening to my favorite CDs, and listening to sermons on TV. It was the lazy kind of day that you can only enjoy in the middle of winter, tucked away in a quiet place, and alone. A light snow had been falling all day, and the wooded area behind the condo was simply breathtaking.

I had been watching the inspirational channel on cable TV and the day had slipped into dusk. The programming was changing to a more infomercial format, so I decided to switch the channel to find a good movie. I stumbled onto HBO just in the beginning of *See Spot Run,* and since I had seen that one with my grandson, I knew it was cute and "safe" for me to watch.

I enjoyed laughing aloud and sighed as the movie ended. I grabbed some chips and came back to the TV to find another movie in progress. I had just missed the title, but I recognized the actors. It was a sequel to the Disney movie *The Mighty Ducks,* which I had also seen and thought to be "safe". I was really hanging out, not trying to be particularly spiritual, and I was also playing "Free Cell" on my laptop. (I know what you fine Christians are thinking by now. What happened to prayer and fasting, right?)

Well, in this movie, the "Ducks" were no longer a team, but many of the players were now on the USA Hockey Team, and they were playing for the championship. They looked a little "sorry" to say the least, and their old coach was trying his best to get this team together. As the movie progressed, we were introduced to the opposing team. It was a tough group from Iceland whose coach had the reputation of being ruthless and unfair. When the teams met in the playoffs, the Iceland team beat the USA team miserably, using every dirty trick they had up their sleeves. The USA team went away defeated, but they got a shot in the arm that gave them hope. They underwent some serious "street training" and learned some new techniques. Their coach went through some new training also, and the team emerged with a new teammate and a new attitude.

Of course, the final playoffs resulted in the USA team having to meet Iceland again. Iceland was tough. They were mean and rough. They did not play fair. They wore black uniforms to intimidate their opponents, and it really worked.

It was now down to the final championship game and the fight was on. Iceland did what they did best, and they were leading by a landslide. Then it was the final period. USA was looking bad and feeling bad, too. The halftime score was embarrassing. The team dragged to the locker room with their heads down. The coach emerged with his last attempt at motivational speaking. He made his pitch. He reminded the team that the easy response to humiliation and inequity is to retaliate, to react, to lose focus of who you are because the opponent is unfairly "whipping up on you". The coach then stepped forward and made everybody announce who they were by name and where they were from. As each team member spoke, the next one gained confidence. They were ultimately yelling their names and where they were from.

Momentum was building as a guest supporter appeared in the locker room. He stepped in to remind them of who they represented and the power of who they really were inside. He even brought new uniforms for them to wear into the game in the final period. They changed their uniforms and confidently raced back into the game.

The USA team went out there and scored consistently. They tied the score, using all their tools, and left no seconds on the clock. The opponents were shocked; they NEVER expected such a comeback. It was now time for the "best of the best" tiebreaker to determine the champions. Each team would have their turn to score, and the opponents were overly confident that they would get the point.

It was down to the wire, and Iceland sent out their best bully. The USA coach sized up the bully (whom he had already been studying) and sent out his weakest-looking contender. It was the girl that this same bully had already aggressively moved on earlier. The coach had carefully studied the bully's moves and knew that the girl was the quickest team member, the least likely to be expected to compete, and, therefore, the best defense against the opponent.

The stage was set. The bully laughed when he saw who his opponent was. He made his moves, and the girl, following the instructions of her coach, anticipated every one of them. The bully HAD to make his point. The game was riding on it.

He made his play with confidence and power! His teammates went wild on the sidelines! It was a good shot! But the girl, in total anticipation, read him like a book and STOPPED THE PLAY! Yeah! The bad guys lost, the game ended, and so did the movie.

As the movie credits began rolling, it showed the team sitting around a campfire, singing "We Are The Champions" (a song by a group called Queen). As I listened to them singing (and, yes, it is a secular song), I seemed to drift off into a place in the Spirit, and I began to praise and moan. I went on, uncontrollably, for some time, while asking God what all the moaning was about. He showed me that we really *are* the champions, and that it was no waste of time to have watched this movie. I think He enjoys showing me deep things from such "shallow" experiences. He wanted me to see that the enemy thinks that he is the champion because he has some power, and he tries to intimidate us into believing that he really is a champion. But the truth of the matter is that *we* are the champions, because God has made us the winners through His Son. Sometimes He has to remind us of who we are, like the defeated team in the locker room. Sometimes He has to send in an extra guest-appearance from the Holy Spirit to encourage us and change our attitude. Sometimes He literally has to change what we are wearing in the middle of the game by stripping off the old mess that no longer fits. But whatever He has to do, we WILL come out as the champions!

But why, you might ask? Because, according to I Samuel 17:47, David reminded Goliath, that self-declared champion, and God reminded the Israelites, His chosen people, that the battle is not ours; it's The Lord's. It does not matter that the enemy may look like giants before us. It does not matter that the enemy may seem to have more power. It does not matter that we seem to have but little strength. What *does* matter is that God has already prepared us for the battle, just as He prepared David as a shepherd. God has already equipped us with weapons we can easily and readily use. And, best of all, God has already promised us the victory. He says the battle is not ours; it is The Lord's, and so it is . . .

CHAPTER X

The Signs Reflect The Law

"And the third day there was a marriage in Cana of Galilee; and the mother of Jesus was there: And both Jesus was called, and his disciples, to the marriage. And when they wanted wine, the mother of Jesus saith unto him, They have no wine. Jesus saith unto her, Woman, what have I to do with thee? mine hour is not yet come. His mother saith unto the servants, Whatsoever he saith unto you, do it."
John 2: 1-5 KJV

The Fourth of July brings many experiences to most of us who live in America, and some of them, I am sure, are so ordinary that under normal circumstances we would dismiss them. Well, I had one such experience on Independence Day right here in Washington, D.C.

It has been my tradition for many years to go down to the Washington Monument to see the fireworks at the close of Independence Day. I raised my children that way, and I have now passed that tradition on to my grandsons and godsons. It can often be a challenge to find a place to park, but that has never discouraged me from this tradition which I simply love to keep. Well, this particular year was no exception, and finding a parking space was a greater challenge than ever before.

I was with my godson and his mom, and we were cruising the downtown northwest quadrant near 17th Street with our eyes peeled. We finally turned onto Pennsylvania Avenue and kept cruising. As we stopped at the light at 20th and Penn, I noticed that a police car was parked on the corner, straddling a perfectly good meter that could have accommodated our minivan. The officer was sitting behind the wheel with several colleagues near

33

the cruiser on foot. It was a display of all the heightened security in our city since 9/11/01. Impulsively, I rolled down the window, called to the officer in the car, and asked him if he would *PLEASE* move the cruiser forward a few feet so that we could get on that meter and be legally parked.

He responded, "No, ma'am."

I went into my begging mode, but he stood his ground. He finally looked across the street and instructed us to pull up behind the last legally parked car. We looked at each other in our vehicle, weighed the instructions for a few seconds, and decided to obey. Once out of our van, we stopped in front of the officer and I blatantly asked if parking on that corner was going to get us in trouble. It was clear that the sign said 'NO PARKING'.

The officer reassured me that he was on duty until midnight, and that unless we were planning to stay beyond midnight, he would see to it that our vehicle was just fine. We walked away, chuckling that we would certainly not be gone past midnight.

As we walked a few feet toward our destination, I was overcome by the spirit of The Lord. I began to yell at my friend that what was happening was really big, that God was showing me something marvelous! Of course, she was waiting to hear what great revelation I had gotten as I began to share what I was seeing. I could not help but recognize that a spiritual principle was being birthed in me. I was keenly aware of the fact that the sign on the corner where we had parked had said 'NO PARKING'. I recognized that the police officer had given us permission to park on that corner. I had his assurance that he would not give us a ticket, not let us get towed away, nor let anything happen to our vehicle. It had hit me like a ton of bricks that even though the sign was clearly reflecting the law and was enforceable if violated, one who is in authority has the power to override the signs and give special liberties to whomever he so

34

desires. I got excited! I thought, *Surely, if a little police officer who does not even make the law has this much power, how much more would my Heavenly Father have who made the law and is the one who enforces it?* I started thinking about the many things in my life that had been granted to me simply because of my Heavenly Father.

But then I went a step further and said, "Now, Lord, it is easy for me to come up with anecdotal evidence, but show me this principle in Your Word." I began to call to mind Scriptures that supported my case, but many of them were times when God had reversed His law of nature, or some other law, to bring to pass a word He had spoken (like Sarah and Elisabeth giving birth) or to advance The Kingdom of God (like raising Lazarus from the dead). Those examples did not satisfy what I was looking for, so I got very specific with The Lord, and I said, "Lord, show me an example where you reversed the law (any law) just to bless somebody, and for no other reason!" After all, there was no reason that we got to safely park our vehicle and go off to enjoy the fireworks, except that God just wanted to bless us! Several Scriptures actually came to mind, believe it or not, and I guess you'll just have to come to hear me in person one day to get them all, but the one that made the case for me is found in John 2. I remembered the marriage feast at Cana of Galilee. If you recall, it was a wedding reception (as we know it today), and at the height of the party the wine ran out. It was one of those occasions that in truth the worst thing that could have happened was that the host would have been highly embarrassed. No one would have died or anything like that. There would just have been some embarrassment.

And what does Jesus do, just because? He totally shakes up the laws of nature and fermentation, or whatever else you want to technically name it, and turns water into wine. I mean, of all things! What could be more non-spiritual! To just give a bunch of people who were already drinking (Remember that the governor of the feast was able to compare good wine to bad.) some more to drink seems just a bit much to me. But because it was important to Jesus' mother who was concerned about her friends, it became important to Jesus. He did a miracle; He changed the way wine was made and made a man look really good before his guests. And why did He do it? Because He wanted to bless him. Boy, oh, boy! That struck a chord with me. Jesus will override laws, signs that reflect the law and the authority of those given to execute the laws, if He wants to! And why? Just to bless ME. Just because He is my Redeemer and I am His child.

Now, all this may seem very silly to you, and maybe even a stretch on the understanding of this whole thing, but I will tell you one thing; you can believe it or not; that's on you, but I choose to believe that my Father loves me like that and that I can receive these miraculous acts. I am excited about Who God is, about who I am in Him, and about how He gives me good gifts even when all the signs say that I cannot have them, that I do not deserve them, and that I had better not even expect them!

All I know is, that in the same manner which the servants took Mary's advice when she gave them instruction, even though there was no way the laws of nature could support filling empty wine vessels, I, too, choose to take her advice today. So even in the midst of the unfavorable, illogical, impassable conditions, or the restriction of the signs before me, I say, "Whatever Jesus says, do it!" If I can follow the seemingly illogical instructions of a little police officer on duty until midnight and expect a good outcome, *surely* I can follow the often "seemingly" illogical instructions of my Heavenly Father. He is on duty past midnight (He neither slumbers nor sleeps.) and has all the authority to back up anything He chooses to change on my behalf!

GLORY!!

CHAPTER XI

God Cares About The Simple Things

"Delight thyself also in the LORD and he shall give thee the desires of thine heart."

Psalm 37:4 (KJV)

The other day I went to get some lunch, and I decided to go to this Vietnamese restaurant in our area that I had not been to before. I walked hesitantly through the entrance doorway and focused on the counter that I could see through the glass window. I paid little attention to the entry past that point. I turned sharply, and to my surprise and embarrassment, I turned right into a glass window. Bam! I bumped my nose. I quickly regrouped, grateful that no one (that I could see) was watching and navigated my way through the door and into the restaurant. My takeout order was ready and waiting, so I paid the young man and left. I did not think much of the incident, except that once outside I looked longingly at the ice cream/Italian-ice stand just to the side of the parking lot. I made a decision that though I really wanted an ice cream/Italian-ice treat, I would probably find some other way to make a mess and do something dumb, so I got into my car and drove the short distance back to work. I had finished my lunch and was pressing through the pile of work on my desk, when one of my colleagues came down the hallway like the "town crier". She was saying, "I'm making a Rita's run. Anybody want anything?"

I could not believe what I was hearing. Rita's was the little ice cream/Italian-ice place that I had opted not to visit. It was such a simple thing, but I knew it was God. He had heard that secret desire of my heart, had watched me bump into that glass barrier, and had heard me decide in my heart that one painful experience

37

into the unknown was all I was willing to venture into for the day. He is so faithful over the least of things that pertain to me that even an unspoken desire for some ice cream did not escape Him. I thought, *Wow, how I really love The Lord,* and I went to share the matter with my colleague. She made it even more exciting when she said, "I don't even know why I did that like that." Being the precious woman of God that she is, she added, "It was just God wanting to bless you."

Well, you might say, "That was a really cute little story," and move on. But don't you dare! I have another one similar to it!

It was on a recent Friday night that I was at church participating in the Friday night youth activities. The youth directors had decided to show the movie *Akeelah and the Bee,* and I had seen it once but had forgotten the ending. It was very near the ending, and suddenly my praise teammates came to see why I was not upstairs in rehearsal. I protested grossly, holding on to the doorframe, pleading shamelessly, but to no avail. I had to go. It was right near the point of the "spell-off" (if you've ever seen the movie), and things were just getting good. I went to rehearsal and let it go.

On the VERY NEXT DAY, I made a 2-hour road trip to see my son, and when I got there, he was not where I could see him. I kept a good attitude and decided to go to his house a few minutes away. When I got to his house, I was greeted by his friend and she invited me to come in. I was there only a few seconds when I realized that their (very big-screen) television was showing a movie. And, yes, you guessed it; it was *Akeelah And The Bee*! And, yes, you guessed it again; it was late in the movie, just a little before the spelling bee started. Can you believe that? A movie that was of NO real significance, but one that I simply wanted to see the ending of was significant to God. And, again, you are probably wondering, "What's the big deal about that?" Well, the big deal is that God is concerned about every detail of my life, and He chooses to bless me about the most ordinary things. And I say, "If He is that faithful over such trivia, how much more faithful will He be over those 'Kingdom things' that I pray about on a regular basis?"

CHAPTER XII

The Banana

"Delight thyself also in the LORD and he shall give thee the desires of thine heart."

Psalm 37:4 (KJV)

It was only two days after my Italian-Ice experience that I had one of those kinds of encounters with God that makes you go, "Hmmm". It was a Saturday morning; I was on my way out the door to go to church for our street evangelism outreach, and clearly He was at it again. It has been my custom for at least the last ten years to start my morning with a banana and some orange juice for breakfast. Anybody who knows me knows that those two items are basics in my diet and in my house. I don't like really ripe bananas, and I tend not to buy them in large quantities so that they will not get too ripe waiting to be eaten. That means, of course, that I have to buy them fairly often to satisfy this little "issue" of mine. I had bought bananas earlier in the week but had eaten my last one on Friday, and I really wasn't feeling like the "grocery store thing" when it was time to head home. As you can imagine, I made a decision to go home without bananas, but thinking I shouldn't.

I awoke on Saturday and made my run down the stairs to get my banana and orange juice, only to remember that I *had* no banana! I resigned myself to my own stupidity and prepared to go to church. I had but opened my front door and turned to lock it, when I noticed a banana lying, no, "placed" on my stoop. It was just lying there, a single banana, and nothing else. I chuckled and looked all around for the owner, waiting for someone to appear. No one appeared, so I then looked up and started shaking my head. "Naw, God," I kept saying, "I can't believe you would do THIS!"

40

I locked the door slowly and waited some more. I then stooped down and slowly picked up the banana. I was still not convinced that it was real. It was ripe, but not too ripe, and it was just the right color and just the right size. I took the banana to church with me, and since I live behind the church, I believed someone on their way in for our outreach had left me a banana. I questioned everyone there, but no one had left the banana. One of the deacons made a joke and said, "I guess it was the banana man."

I responded that He had been called many things in my life, so why not "The banana man". I could not help but think about my decision not to go to the store when I knew I should have gone, and then about my desire to have a banana for breakfast that I could not satisfy. I kept on thinking, though, while excited about my God and how wonderful He is, how marvelously He takes care of me, and how He truly is the Great I AM. I had started my morning in worship, delighting myself in Him, making up worship medleys, and just having fun basking in His Presence. What did He do in return? He gave me the desires of my heart. Pretty simple and quite a good deal, I might add. I'll have to remember this the next time I am in a tougher situation. If I keep delighting myself in Him, He will keep doing what His Word says He will do! WOW!

Oh, by the way, if you are wondering if I ate that strange banana from that unknown source; you bet I did!! It was heavenly!!

CHAPTER XIII

The Fire In My Bed

"But now thus saith the LORD that created thee, O Jacob, and he that formed thee, O Israel, Fear not: for I have redeemed thee, I have called thee by name; thou art mine. When thou passeth through the waters, I will be with thee; and through the rivers, they shall not overflow thee: when thou walkest through the fire, thou shall not be burned; neither shall the flame kindle upon thee."

Isaiah 43:1,2 (KJV)

Many years ago, when my oldest son was of elementary-school age and my middle son was a toddler, my husband worked at night in a nearby city. During those days (partly because I was young) I could somehow stay up half the night and still manage to function as if I'd had plenty of sleep. I was an avid reader and would sometimes read one novel in one night. Since my husband would be at work, my staying up to read did not bother him at all, and it was a great way to give me some company.

On one of those nights, I was reading and had obviously become more tired than at other times. My bedroom was designed so that the nightstand and the lamp were just immediately to the right of my right arm. We were not very wealthy and our furnishings were not going to win any major competitions in the decorator world. Our lamp, sitting at the edge of the stand, was a little lamp with one of those pop-on shades. It was placed just in reach of my hand for my convenience. I had fallen asleep and must have been sleeping soundly, having failed to turn off the light and bed down properly. At some point in my sleep, I heard someone call my name. The whisper was so gentle and sweet. It simply said "Paulette". So I woke up, not in terror or in anguish, but rather peacefully, and I sat up. When I sat up, I noticed that my lamp was not on the stand, but it was lodged between the stand and the mattress and that the shade was on the floor.

As I adjusted myself to being awake, I smelled a strange smell like fabric burning and realized that my mattress was on fire. I jumped out of the bed and looked back. My mattress was in a calm smolder, but more unbelievably, my pillow had already begun to burn. I looked at that pillow in total amazement because it had burned all around my head and etched around my hairline. My hair, which was about shoulder length, had been loose and sprawled all over that pillow in no reasonable order. The fire had burned all around the edges of my hair, but not one hair on my head had been burned. It literally looked like an old 'Etch-O-Sketch' drawing that my children would have made.

As I studied the scene in total awe, I recognized that the mattress, too, was burning right in the spot where I had fallen asleep. I then knew that it had been the Spirit of The Lord who had called my name and had caused me to wake up.

I jumped into gear without much thought. Calling the fire department never even crossed my mind. I ran to the closet, got towels, and wet them. I stuffed them under my two sons' door where they were sleeping soundly. I grabbed the mattress and began pulling it off the bed, down the hall, and out the patio door. I ran back and checked the boys' door to make sure no smoke could get in and sat down in the middle of the floor to cry. I knew I could not reach my husband at that hour because he worked in a factory and would not be able receive a call. Then I thought, *Oh, the fire department.*

So I called the fire department and my dad. My dad was very shaken and of course asked about the fire department. I mentioned that I had just called them and, of course, *again* got the scolding of my life. The fire department came to the apartment with all their equipment in the middle of the night, and I met them at the door with a bit of an attitude. My instructions were that they had better not tear up my house and they'd better get outside on the patio if they wanted to see any fire. Once they saw that there was no danger, they gave me a lecture on "How to respond to a fire in your home" and left.

When I think back on that night, I still marvel at how much God loves me and protects me from the "seen and unseen" dangers. But I also think about how His Plans and Purpose for me cannot be thwarted by the enemy or even by my own foolishness. I rest easy in knowing that the PURPOSE OF GOD SHALL STAND. Further, I stand confident in knowing that MY GOD is able to keep the heat out of fire, and that if I had to stand by the three Hebrew boys and give testimony, mine would be just as awesome as theirs!

CHAPTER XIV

The Flowers In Kazakhstan

"Now there cried a certain woman of the wives of the sons of the prophets unto Elisha, saying Thy servant my husband is dead; and thou knowest that thy servant did fear the Lord: and the creditor is come to take unto him my two sons to be bondmen.

And Elisha said unto her, What shall I do for thee? Tell me what hast thou in the house? And she said, Thine handmaid hath not anything in the house, save a pot of oil.

Then he said, Go borrow thee vessels abroad of all thy neighbors, even empty vessels, borrow not a few.

And when thou art come in, thou shalt shut the door upon thee and upon thy sons, and shalt pour out into all those vessels, and thou shalt set aside that which is full.

6 And it came to pass, when the vessels were full, that she said unto her son, Bring me yet a vessel, And he said unto her, There is not a vessel more. And the oil stayed."

II Kings 4:1-4, 6 (KJV)

Back in 2001, just after 9/11, I was scheduled to take a mission trip with an Aglow team of seven to Kazakhstan. It was in October and people were understandably very fearful of traveling. Our team leader assessed the situation and decided we would move forward. All of us, from different parts of the country, decided that she was right.

We had been ministering to a women's group of a few hundred women in a small, very-poor village, and it was nearly time to go. The village leaders wanted to bless us but of course could not pay us money, so they brought in a bouquet of carnations, separated them, and gave each of us a flower. There were seven Americans and about three or four local ladies working with us. We all received our flowers and got loaded into our little mini-bus headed for our next stop to end our day of ministry. We were going to the women's prison. Our driver was a young man with a fairly new wife, and he really wanted to take his wife flowers, too. In our "girlie compassion", we gave him flowers for his wife, which he safely tucked alongside the driver's seat lest we inadvertently forget that they were not ours.

Once at the prison we discovered that we would not be able to go inside, so, after some discussion, a few women were allowed to come out to the yard where we were. We were very saddened to see that some women had their small children in prison with them. As we ministered, one woman received The Lord as Savior, and in celebration, whomever was praying decided she would go to the van, get her flower, and give it to the woman. After that, a few more women came, then a few more, and they all wanted flowers. We could not very well say no, and we refused to take back the flowers already given, so we made an unconscious decision that we would give all our flowers away. The problem came when we continued to see those women who still had no flower, and we knew our supply should be dried up too soon. But we kept going back to the van every time we needed another flower, and every time we went to get one, there would be another one there.

We really had no idea how many women received flowers that day, and we even tried to reason that the count must have included the driver's stash. But we quickly discovered that the driver had not let his stash get away, and we then began to try to figure out what God had done. What we do know is that every time we reached for a flower, there was one, and when the last woman in that prison that came to us got a flower, there were no more. WE KNEW, WITHOUT A DOUBT, THAT THE FLOWER WE TOOK OFF THAT SEAT WAS THE LAST ONE, EACH TIME!

And yet there would always be another and another. When the last woman received her flower, we reached in, but there was nothing more. It was just like that widow's oil that kept coming until the last jar was filled in II Kings 4, and the Bible says in verse 6 that when the last pot was filled, "the oil stayed". I will never forget that day, nor will I soon forget that MY GOD SHALL SUPPLY ALL MY NEEDS ACCORDING TO HIS RICHES IN GLORY THROUGH CHRIST JESUS.

CHAPTER XV

The Knot On My Son's Head

"Then he called his twelve disciples together, and gave them power and authority over all devils, and to cure diseases. And he sent them to preach the kingdom of God, and to heal the sick ..."

Luke 9:1,2 (KJV)

It was right around my birthday in the middle of July, a hot summer day in Washington, D.C. I was parenting five young children at that time, and they were ALWAYS doing SOMETHING! I had allowed them to go outside to play with the neighborhood children. They were out having fun and I was inside, grateful for the break. They were playing with a scooter up and down the block, along with many other silly games that kept them mobile. I looked out, thinking how sweaty they would be when they came inside and that baths would be the next order of business.

I remember seeing the crowd blast past our gate toward the other end of the street when I heard the cries and screams of panic. I rushed out the door and down to the mob of children. My stepson had fallen while fast in motion and had banged and scraped his forehead. He had a big knot and a gaping spot that was oozing fresh blood.

Now, the really timely thing about this day is that it was not very long after I'd had an encounter with the Holy Spirit which had changed my life. I had met Him in a powerful new way, and I was downright silly! I just believed God! I had not had time for the well-meaning "church folk" to tell me I was too radical or that I

48

should calm down because "it didn't take all that!" So when I saw that big knot (that I really did not want to have to explain to that child's natural mother) I got mad! I took one look at the situation, reached out, laid hands on my stepson's head, and called on the Name of Jesus. In an INSTANT, the skin on that child's head went back to normal, the knot disappeared, and everything returned to the way it had been before.

The other children (including my own) stood there with their mouths open, looking at me like I was an alien. They all made some sounds of something close to fear and amazement. I checked things out. Things looked fine. I went on back into the house praising my God. The children marveled over that day for many years to come, but, boy, did they learn about the power of God (OK, I did, too.). It was at that point that I KNEW that God would do what His Word said He would do, and more than that, He would do it FOR ME!

Paulette Pierce Holloway

CHAPTER XVI

My Day In Court

"Behold I send you forth as sheep in the midst of wolves: be ye therefore wise as serpents, and harmless as doves. And you shall be brought before governors and kings for my sake, for a testimony against them and the Gentiles. But when they deliver you up, take no thought how or what you shall speak: for it shall be given you in that same hour what ye shall speak."

Matthew 10:16, 18,19 (KJV)

My oldest son has made those choices over the years that break a mother's heart. He has gotten involved with criminal behavior which has cost him much of his freedom. He, alone, is never the only victim of the tragic waste of life, but in this case, his son has suffered tremendously, as well.

It was the summer of my 30-year class reunion, and I found myself in the town not far from where my grandson lived. He was visiting with his "other" grandmother, and she called me to come see the child. I witnessed signs of physical abuse and immediately called the authorities. I decided that my grandson would not continue to suffer, even though his father was not there to protect him.

Some months later, I received a notice that my grandson's mother had filed a petition with the court, requesting that his father and none of his father's family have any legal rights to be in contact with this child. The thought of such an action just broke my heart, and I could not imagine what would happen to him if we were not involved in some way. A hearing was set, but my son was still incarcerated and would have no way to attend. I began to talk to my Heavenly Father about the situation and asked Him if He would intervene.

50

The decision to drive down to the hearing some two hours away seemed to be the clearest thing to do. My middle son and I made the trip, not knowing what to expect but believing that God would do SOMETHING!

We got to the court and waited for the case to be called. Once called, we all went into the courtroom. My grandson was in school and not present for the hearing, but his mom and her friend were there. The judge looked around the courtroom and asked who we all were. I told him who I was, and he wanted to know why I was there. I explained that the child's father was not able to attend the hearing and that I was there to make sure my grandson was kept safe. The judge quickly informed me that grandparents had no rights in these matters, and I responded that I understood. He proceeded with questioning my grandson's mom, and things just started happening. I never made any more comments in that hearing, but after the judge had listened and had asked many questions, he asked her if I was a threat to the child. Well, of course I was not, so he asked why I could not see the child. The response did not seem to satisfy the judge, so he turned to me and asked if I would like visitation.

"Of course, I would," I responded.

He ordered visitation for me at my convenience, ordered that the child be assigned an attorney to protect the child's rights, and ordered that I be prepared to testify at the next hearing as to the cooperative (or not) way in which the court's orders were being executed. He then set a review date and asked me to get my calendar and tell him what was good for me. I stood there in total amazement, trying to figure out what had just happened. I had said NOTHING to plead my case. I had made NO attempts to manipulate any circumstances prior to the hearing. I had not been mean or malicious toward the child's mother. BUT GOD! He'd heard my cry; He'd fought my battle; He'd delivered, and

51

He'd given me more than anything I could have asked for or imagined! And He continues to take care of my grandson far better than I ever could! I know that all I have to do is trust Him. He is trustworthy and a keeper of His Word! And, yes, like the old folk say, "He's a lawyer in a courtroom."

CHAPTER XVII
The Ham Juice

"Then saith he to the man, Stretch forth thine hand.
And he stretched it forth; and it was restored whole, like as
the other."

Matthew 12:13 (KJV)

It was a Saturday night during the era when I had recently begun to experience the power of God in my life. Most any Saturday night at our house meant that I was in the kitchen cooking my Sunday dinner. Being from the South, I still had that old tradition of not cooking on Sundays and of enjoying being able to eat soon after you come home from church. My five children were in the other room entertaining themselves, and my husband was sitting at the kitchen table talking and keeping me company. I was boiling a ham and preparing the rest of my meal. It was time to turn the ham over because it had been on one side long enough, so I interrupted the rest of my duties to attend to the ham.

I took my long turning fork, speared the ham, and proceeded to turn it. About halfway through my production, the ham slipped off the fork. The ham fell back into the pot and made a big splash, and the boiling-hot juice from the pot splashed out and onto my hand.

I cannot tell you ANYTHING that I have ever experienced which came close to that kind of pain. The hot water, weighted with grease from the ham, splashed and stuck to my hand, burning it deeply and instantly. The pain from the burn was so excruciating that I nearly lost my balance. It felt as if someone was boring through my hand with a hot drill. The skin peeled off my hand just as if a strong wind was blowing on it. My head was throbbing because of the pain, and my screams filled the house. My husband jumped out of his chair and came toward me, but he was looking helpless. I could hear the children starting to run in our direction.

Without thinking about it, really just merely reacting to it, I swiped my good hand across my burned one and cried out, "Be healed in Jesus' Name!"

Just as instantly as the skin had peeled off my hand, it unpeeled and smoothed back out! There was NO EVIDENCE of my hand having been burned! My husband fell backward in awe, and the children entered only to find my hand completely restored. The only thing remaining was the pain. The hand had been healed so quickly that it seemed as though my brain had not gotten the message of this miraculous event, and it was still registering that I should be in pain. It was a few hours before all the pain subsided, but today, I dare you to try to figure out which hand was burned. I cannot remember, nor can I tell. I believe it was the right hand because I am right handed and that would be logical, but I cannot tell by the way it looks.

All I do know is that there is POWER in the Name of Jesus. There is HEALING in the Name of Jesus. There is RESTORATION in the Name of Jesus. And if you call on Him, He will answer!!

CHAPTER XVIII
Fire In The Washer

"And say unto him, Take heed, and be quiet; fear not, neither be fainthearted for the two tails of these smoking firebrands, ... Thus saith the Lord GOD, It shall not stand, neither shall it come to pass."

Isaiah 7:4a,7 (KJV)

I was going through a particularly hard time in my life, adjusting to having my daughter, who I had raised from the age of two, taken from me unexpectedly after nine years and returned to her natural parents. She had been challenged in many ways during that absence from me and had endured more than any eleven year old should. She had been living with her father for nearly one year, and she was then found without a safe place to go. During that time, I had moved into a two-bedroom condo with two of my sons because my life, too, was in great transition. The one surety in my life during that season was my increased desire for God and for walking out my faith every day. As a matter of fact, it had become somewhat of a joke with my sons that I seemed to constantly be on a "Mission" of some sort for "The Kingdom". I was honored that I could have such a reputation.

I had discovered that my daughter was once again in distress, so I stepped up to the plate and received her back into my home. My living situation had changed, and I really did not have a bedroom for her, but I knew that we would make some sacrifices to do what needed to be done. She, too, had changed and was wounded and sad. She was grateful to have returned to me, but she was very angry about all the disruptions in her life.

There was a constant battle in our home over who was in charge. Understand that there was no "question" about who was in charge, only the battle that comes when authority is constantly challenged. We struggled for many months, but my faith grew stronger, and I grew more determined to stand firm against the attacks of the enemy.

Our challenge was often in the morning when it was time for my daughter to go to school so that I could get to work on time, and this particular morning was typical. She refused to go out the door; I insisted she go out the door. She refused to go out the door; I insisted she go out the door. After several volleys back and forth that morning, I got REALLY mad at the devil for messing with ME and MY CHILD! I decided that enough was enough and that he had to GO! So I stopped responding to the child and started addressing the spirit that was "in my face". It did not take much of the "Name of Jesus and the Blood of Jesus" for that foul spirit to get the message and find someone else's house to terrorize. My daughter was transformed into the compliant, sweet child that she had been known to be and then went to school.

That would seem like a nice ending to a great story, right? Well, by now, I'm sure you know better than that! As was my custom of practicing "time management 101", I had been doing some laundry while making lunches, while preparing the kids for school, and so on. The washer was chugging away and should have been ready to bring its cycle to an end. I turned back to my duties at hand only to recognize that the washer had stopped and there was no spin. Thinking that odd, I went to the closet that housed the stacked washer/dryer, lifted the lid on the washer, and flames leaped out at me. I dropped the lid and jumped back as quickly as you can imagine and regrouped. *What in the world is going on? How can the washer be on fire while it is full of water?*

Flames were surrounding the tub that was full of water and clothes, but nothing inside the tub was being burned. I grabbed the fire extinguisher from the kitchen and rushed back to the washer, opened the lid, and shot solution all around the flames. Nothing! More flames! I dropped the lid and ran to call the fire department.

Then, all of a sudden, I remembered the events of my morning, and I thought, *Aha! Retaliation! Well, I don't think so!* I began running through the rooms of the condo that were closest to the closet and laying my hands on the walls. I was yelling, "Devil, you didn't buy nothing in here, and you can't burn nothing!" I was calling on the Name of My God and speaking protection over our home. I spoke to those flames and dared them to expand, and I kept running through the house while thanking God for His Divine Protection. When I think back on it now, I imagine that I would have looked pretty crazy to anyone taping my behavior, and it makes me chuckle.

In a few minutes the fire department was there, and about five men charged through my door with hoses. I stopped them abruptly and told them that the fire was in the washer in the closet and that they had better not tear up my house for that little fire. They went right to work spraying their solution on the fire. The flames got higher. They tried a few more things that I cannot really describe, because they made me wait over near the balcony and out of the way. After many minutes and many different types of efforts, they stood back, totally puzzled. They admitted that they had never seen anything like it before. They had never even seen an electrical fire not respond to ANYTHING! Finally, they concluded that they would have to remove the entire washer and get it out of the house.

The fire was still going strong, so they worked on their strategy not to have the flames burn them while they transported the washer. I offered that they had better make sure my clothes did not burn either, so they began taking the dripping wet clothes out and putting them in a container which I had provided.

57

By now I was beginning to see something bigger going on, so I start singing softly and praising my God. I was sitting on the sofa just observing them and sweetly singing songs of praise. The firemen started chatting with me and making remarks about my behavior and attitude. One of them sat down on the other end of my sofa and just laid back on the sofa like he was AT HOME, while his colleagues got the washer disconnected and maneuvered it out of that closet. In a few minutes they had gotten the washer free, while the flames continued to leap around every time they opened the lid. They managed to get the washer through my living room, through the balcony doors, and onto the balcony.

We all stood looking either through the doorway or were on the balcony, and we were all amazed by what happened next. One of the firemen opened the lid as soon as the washer was placed on the balcony. The flames leaped forward in a big gush and went out! They literally disappeared. Puff! Gone! We all looked at each other and made our way back into the living room, making no comment for fear of the explanation (or lack thereof).

I then had four or five men milling around in my house. No one was doing much talking, and no one seemed as if they were trying to leave. Finally, one of them asked me if I played the piano that was sitting there. I responded that I played a little. Then one of them said, "It feels really peaceful in here; what is going on? I don't want to leave."

I jokingly said, "You're going out of here, because I have to go to work. I'm already over an hour late." But he was serious, and I knew that the Spirit of The Lord was so strong in my home that others could sense His Presence. I finally did get those men out of my house, and I went to work later that day, but for a little while after they were gone, I sat quietly, reflecting on how awesome God is. I could honestly say that whatever comes against me is subject to the authority of MY GOD, even FIRE. The morning had started with a spiritual power struggle, then it had gotten a little ugly, or should I say, "Hot", and it ended with all that stuff submitting to the power of the Living God. Now who can mess with that?

CHAPTER XIX
The Blow Dryer

"No weapon that is formed against thee shall prosper;"
Isaiah 54:17a (KJV)

In 2006 I was scheduled to be one of the speakers at an annual women's luncheon for yet another year. The luncheon always starts on a Saturday morning and goes through the afternoon, and I don't ever seem to have time leading up to that day to get my personal details taken care of. Well, this time was no exception, and I had not been able to pull off getting to the hairstylist so that at least my hair could look good. (I know; vanity, vanity, all is vanity.) It had been a busy week and Friday night had just sneaked up on me. *Now what? I guess I'll just have to wash my hair and make me a nice French roll.*

I set out as always, regretting that I was having to style my own hair AGAIN, but I went ahead with the inevitable. A part of my dread is that I had a blow dryer that I bought at Montgomery Ward's way before they went out of business. I'm sure that it had enough asbestos in it for me to start a small chemical war. The next unexciting piece of news was that the cord plug was too bulky to really fit into my bathroom outlet securely, and it was constantly falling out with the motion of my brushing my wet hair. To eliminate the second problem, I decided that I would simply take the dryer to another room, use an extension cord, and give myself plenty of wiggle room for my task.

I had managed to wash my hair without the need to take off my gold bracelet, earrings, or gold necklace. After all, I never have to remove those things when I go the stylist. I was now wet-haired and poised to get done the job at hand. I plugged the extension cord into the outlet, and then I plugged the blow dryer into the extension cord. Somehow, when I forced the plug into the extension cord, the cord fell apart and only exposed wires were there. I was holding the blow dryer in my hand that had the bracelet, and my wet hair was dripping onto my earrings and necklace. Suddenly, a jolt of electricity shot from that plug, traveled up and down my arm, and then across my chest! It shook me so hard that I stumbled backward. I dropped everything and just stood there totally stunned. Once I realized what had happened and that I had just been electrocuted, I got MAD!

I yelled, "Okay, Devil, so what if I am dumb! So what that I shouldn't have been so careless! How dare you try to kill me? I AM, TOO, going to give this word tomorrow. YOU ARE STUPID!! I shall not die, but live. I shall go forth and declare the Works of The Lord!" I started running through my house yelling at the top of my voice! I was laying hands on myself, yelling the Word, laughing, shaking my head at how dumb I can be, how stupid the Devil is, and how faithful God is. I thought how foolish that headline would have read: 'Intelligent Woman Uses Faulty Extension Cord To Blow-Dry Wet Hair While Wearing Metal.'

Well, all I could do was praise God and tell the Devil how stupid he is, thinking that he would get to capitalize on my foolishness. Didn't he KNOW? No weapon formed against me shall PROSPER. I am NOT dying until EVERYTHING that God has purposed for me gets done. And he, El Stupido, Dumbo, the Idiot, might as well get used to that!

Now, on a more humble note, I really did learn my lesson and have become very cautious about important safety matters, and I encourage you to do the same. From a spiritual perspective, though, the experience only confirmed what I already knew, and that is that NOTHING can compare to the faithfulness of My God!

61

CHAPTER XX

Keys At The Airport

"Behold, the eye of the LORD is upon them that fear him, upon them that hope in his mercy."
Psalm 33:18 (KJV)

Over the years, I regret that I have had to live fairly independently and without a lot of day to day help in getting things done. I tend to be very logical (most times), and I reason way too much. By the time I think I might need to ask someone for help, I conclude that I can just figure out the plan and go make it happen. Some of that may be pride or not wanting to ask for help, and some of it is definitely learned behavior because of the circumstances and people I have had in my world. Whatever the cause, it seems to be the way I have become (But I *am* working on it!).

For example, if I need to go to the airport, I either jump on the train and go, or I choose to park my car in the long-term parking lot and just pay the fee when I exit. (No matter that when other folks need to go to the airport, they just ask me for a ride.) I hate to inconvenience people to do things for me that I perceive I can do for myself. And again, because of my logical thinking, I perceive that I can figure out a plan for MOST things.

Now, with all that said, let me tell you what happened. I had to make a short, three-day trip (which was all-the-more reason that I could justify parking in the lot) to Knoxville, TN. I remember mentioning to a friend that I was going on a trip, and he asked how I was going to get to the airport. Though his question was asked very nicely and with no apparent baggage attached, I retorted that I was going to drive my car and park in the long-term parking lot (with a slight bit of arrogance at the possible implication that I needed some help). He remained patient and said that it was

62

acceptable for me to just get a ride. I was not going to even consider such an offer and said so. It was silly and certainly inconvenient for him, OR ANYONE, when all I had to do was drive.

The time came for me to travel, and I drove myself to the airport as planned, parked my car, and went to the shuttle stop to catch the shuttle bus to the terminal. As soon as I sat down to prepare myself to board the shuttle, I saw it coming and jumped up. I boarded the bus, got to the terminal, and made my flight with ease.

I returned from Knoxville to the DC airport at the appointed time, only to discover that there was a major unexpected weather emergency and all the neighboring airports had been closed. People were packed in the airport everywhere, trying to get to their destinations. I made my way through the crowd and found me a spot near the restrooms to search my purse for my keys so I could then climb aboard the shuttle bus. I could not find my keys. I then sat down under people's legs, opened my luggage, and searched there, thinking that maybe I had tossed them in there while I was away. They were not to be found.

Well, Miss Logical did not panic. I had an extra key in the secret compartment of my purse, so I decided to use that to get into my car, and then take my time in the sanctity of the car to search my purse and luggage more carefully.

I got on the shuttle and arrived at my destination. I found my car easily, and with my spare key in hand, I proceeded to activate the unlock button. When I approached my passenger-side door, I noticed a white sheet of paper on my driver's seat. I knew that was odd, because if you knew ANYTHING about me, you would know that I am organized and have a place for everything and WOULD NOT leave a piece of paper on my seat! I opened my car and picked up the paper to read a note from a stranger saying that they had found my keys at Bus Shelter #14 and had turned them in at the security office.

63

I sat down in the car in amazement, because, first of all, I did not know I had lost the keys, and secondly, how did the note get INSIDE the correct car? Then my logical, analytical mind kicked in, and I began to piece things together.

When I had sat down at the bus shelter to regroup and saw the bus coming, I still had my keys in my hand. I had obviously laid them down to organize things, and when I saw the bus, I rushed away without looking back. Some person had come along behind me and had seen my keys. That person had to have pushed the panic button on my key ring and caused my car to identify itself. Once they spotted my car, which would obviously have been near the shelter where I had boarded the bus, they simply went to my car and opened it.

Now, I need you to stop right here and shout with me! Do you believe that? In Washington D.C., there is a person who has the keys to your car and does not take the car. They do NOT take your car to your house because there is identifying information in your glove compartment which clearly shows your address. They do not burglarize your house and take your "stuff", knowing full well that you could NEVER identify who they are. This is the same Washington D.C. where people are afraid to leave their cars at these lots because of theft and burglary right there on the lots! Okay, keep on shouting while you read.

I got into my car, weeping and thanking God for His Goodness to me and proceeded to the exit. Once at the exit, I asked about my keys and was informed that they would have been turned in to the police sub-station after 24 hours. The attendant recommended that I re-park my car, catch the shuttle back to the terminal, and go to the police sub-station, because parking in front of the terminal would be impossible.

I followed her advice and went back to the terminal. I now had invested about ninety minutes in this little adventure. I found the police sub-station and walked up to the counter to make my case. The police officer was very nice, looked for the keys, but did not have them. He asked how long it had been, and I told him three days, so he apologetically said to me that after 48 hours things are sent to the lost-and-found office. I thanked him and asked for directions. He apologized again and said that office closed at 4:00 P.M. on Fridays, and it was now close to 7:00. I paused and smiled at him. I thanked him and told him to have a wonderful evening and that I was going home until I could get back on Monday.

He stared at me and said, "That's it? Lady, you're just going to tell me to have a wonderful evening? Do you know that I have been cursed out because flights are cancelled, bags are lost, rental-car places have no more cars, and the snow has NO business falling during this time of year! And you're just going to walk away, after all that it seems you have been through today? Well, lady, you have made my day. I am calling my wife and telling her this one. You have a wonderful evening, too."

I went back to my car and went home. I did call my friend to tell him my story, but he refrained from saying, "I told you so," because he could clearly see the Favor of God all over this one. On Monday, I called the attendant in Lost and Found. I explained my situation and identified my keys. He told me I could come anytime. He marveled at my story, because you know I had to tell him, too.

When I got there to pick up my keys, he had told his colleague my story, and they were both marveling at how impossible the outcome was. We all knew that it was not an ordinary outcome. What I do know with a certainty is that the Eyes of The Lord are upon them who fear Him. He had His Eye on me and on my property the WHOLE time. He gave me favor beyond measure and proved HIMSELF to me just one more time. How can I not serve HIM?

65

CHAPTER XXI

My Birthday Party

"The eyes of the LORD are upon the righteous, and his ears are open unto their cry."

Psalm 34:15 KJV

I love birthdays! I think that everyone should celebrate their birthday. It is God's gift to you and can only be celebrated if you are ALIVE. So, if you are alive, my philosophy is that you have reason to celebrate. Now, personally, I try to celebrate my birthday for the entire month of July, just to make sure God knows how grateful I am for my life. My birthday is July 11, and I made a personal commitment about 25 years ago that July 11 would be a National Holiday and that I should not work on that day! Well, this year was no exception, and I made my usual plan to be off. Sometimes, I will let someone else in on the plan, but sometimes I don't. It depends on my mood. Having people around can be nice sometimes, and being alone can also be nice sometimes. So plans vary from year to year. This year, I had not firmed up any plans yet when I received a communication that I needed to conduct a training session on that day.

I serve as an adoption trainer for our state along with two other trainers. Agencies contact the national office and make a request for a training, and we schedule dates for training at our convenience. One of my colleagues had scheduled a training for July 11 (I guess that since July 11 isn't her birthday, it was alright.) and now had a serious family emergency that would prohibit her from being able to do the training. Our other colleague had, just days earlier, taken a new job and would no longer be able to serve as a trainer. The office knew nothing else to do but to contact me, because getting a training pulled together is a major feat involving many people, and to cancel would not have been wise. After

66

much whining and unproductive negotiation attempts, I agreed to conduct the training.

When my birthday arrived, I changed the message on my home phone to let all my well-wishers know that I would be out of the loop during most of the day, but that they had BETTER leave me my birthday greetings anyway (OK, so I'm a bit neurotic.). That surprised no one, I am sure, because I will usually change the message on my birthday so that anyone who calls will know it is my birthday, just in case they had forgotten. I kept my cellphone on until it was absolutely forbidden, so that I could get as many actual voices as possible (Pathetic, I know; I know.)

I made it to the training site and unpacked my car with a bit of an attitude, but I was not REAL bad. I told all of the folks helping me that it was my birthday.

Once the training started in this room full of strangers, I told them that it was my birthday and that I was working on my birthday for the first time in many years. They all felt really sorry for me and told me, "Happy Birthday". I got over myself and went on with doing my job. I enjoy training and I really know my subject matter, so this really was a fun day for me, despite all my whining.

We took our usual break in the morning, so I turned my cellphone on, and, sure enough, someone had called to wish me a happy birthday. We made it until lunch and I turned my phone on again. Yes, more calls.

The class was having their lunch (We provide a catered lunch to control the time.) and we were nearing the end of lunchtime when one of the participants asked everyone to stand. I looked up to see what was going on, because I was "in charge", and I knew that this was not a normal part of my day. As I looked up, two of the participants came into the room with a birthday cake covered with candles, singing, "Happy Birthday To You". Another person gave me a card that had been signed by all the participants. They just giggled and clapped and watched my face. They wanted to have a party I my honor. Someone took my cellphone and took a picture of me and my cake.

I just stood there with tears in my eyes. I could not believe how much God loved me. All I had done was whine and act childish, but He had rewarded the deep places of my heart in spite of me. God had stirred it in the hearts of those strangers to make my day special. Can you believe that? It was the absolute, best birthday party I have ever had, a party thrown by My Daddy, my Abba Father.

I thought about that day for weeks, marveling at how much God cares, even about the silly little things in our hearts. I later thought about how much of God's Heart I would have missed if I had not worked on that birthday, so I am learning to whine less and to just go with the order that He has set for my day!

CHAPTER XXII

Move Your Car

"But I say unto you, Love your enemies, bless them that curse you, do good to them that hate you, and pray for them which despitefully use you, and persecute you;"
Matthew 5:44 (KJV)

It was a typical day for me. I had made an appointment at the hairstylist, and, as usual, I did not have enough time to do all that I needed to do and still get there on time. I really do not like being late, so I will often rush around once I see that time is not on my side. Today, I was rushing. I had begun to ask The Lord for help in finding a place to park so as not to waste unnecessary time by circling the block. I pulled up on the corner near the entrance to the hair salon. There was about a half-a car length of space to park without being too close to the car in front of me, but the 'NO PARKING' sign was about midway of my car. I took the partial space and peered ahead into the car in front of me, because I could see a good amount of space between that car and the next one ahead.

THANK YOU, GOD, there was a person in the car in front of me. I hopped out of my car with enthusiasm and bounced to the passenger side of the car, and, seeing that the window open, I bent down to speak and make my request. I greeted the lady in my sweetest "I love Jesus" voice and with my BEST smile. I explained to her that I needed to park, and I asked her if she was able to move up just a little so that I could get the end of my car within the sign.

She told me, "No," and looked away. I stood there, not believing that she would not move her car up just a few feet for me to park. I graciously thanked her anyway and went into the beauty parlor, perplexed and asking The Lord to PLEASE protect my car for the 90 minutes I would be in with the hairstylist.

69

When I entered the shop, there were several women being served by other stylists, and as my stylist asked how I was doing, I discovered that I was more disturbed about what had just happened than I'd had time to process, because I began recounting to her what had just happened. Even while I was talking, though, I made a conscious decision that I was not going to let that lady get to me, and I found myself making a rather loud declaration that I was going to bless that woman anyway and not curse her. Many of the women in the shop heard me and smiled as if to say, "Yeah, lady, but nobody is *that* spiritual."

My stylist got me to the bowl, and no sooner had she gotten my hair under the water than did a knock come at the door. When the door was opened, a little girl came in and asked, "Where is the lady who just came in here? My mother said to tell her that she is sorry and she will move her car now."

A hush came over the salon. My stylist responded, "Here she is, and I will let her up so she can come out." She wrapped a towel around my head, and I ran outside. I moved my car to within legal lines and paused to thank the lady. She started offering me some kind of an explanation about why she had not moved when I'd asked her, but I interrupted her, assuring her that no explanation was necessary and that I truly appreciated her. I waved and scurried back into the shop. Once inside, I heard the many conversations of amazement and felt so good in my heart that I had been a good witness for "The Kingdom" that day.

CHAPTER XXIII
No Food To Eat

*"I have been young, and now am old: yet have I not seen
the righteous forsaken, nor his seed begging bread."*
Psalm 37:25 (KJV)

A few years ago, I was asked by my employer to join a team on a special project that would require my being flown to our National Office in Grand Rapids, MI, in the middle of the winter. When I got to Grand Rapids it was snowing (at least to me; the locals said it was "lake effect"), and the situation looked pretty grave to me. As no one else seemed to be concerned about the weather (no matter that I was the only woman in this group) the meeting went on as scheduled. Once the meeting was over, I was given a ride to the hotel that was to accommodate me for the next two days. I had been scheduled to stay for two days because it was more cost effective than flying for one day.

Once secure inside the hotel and still watching the buildup of snow from the "lake effect", I started thinking about what I might do for dinner. I had been given lunch at the meeting, so I was not hungry just yet, just planning ahead. The hotel did not have a restaurant, only a breakfast area. There was a decent restaurant next door that I had frequented many times before on other business occasions in Grand Rapids, so walking there seemed like a good tentative plan.

I took a short nap and awoke to find things looking dark outside. It was only 5:00 P.M., so why was it so dark? I had only been in my room for less than an hour. Well, that "lake effect" had kept on falling, snow drifts had mounted, and snow had actually covered much of my first floor window. This did not look good even to an independent-thinking, take-care-of-myself optimist like me.

I made my way down and around to the front desk and asked the clerk if what was happening was normal. No, it was not. The snow drifts had gotten so high that travel was very minimal and most businesses had closed. She did not expect any relief for her to even be able to go home at the end of her shift. She was certain that the restaurant next door was closed.

Things were not sounding good for me, because I had another day before my flight, and I was now starting to think about how hungry I would be by then. My only consoling thought was that there would at least be breakfast in the morning. I asked the clerk if there was any breakfast stuff lurking around in the back, but she said she did not have access to the locked area.

Now I am getting worried and starting to feel REALLY hungry. I thought about the vending machines I had seen near the stairs as I'd come down the corridor and started counting my change in my mind. I did not think I had enough to do much good.

At around 7:00 p.m., I decided that I would try the vending machine and found enough snacks to keep me from feeling hungry, but I still wanted something substantial. I got tea from the breakfast area and went back to my room and read a little, trying not to be preoccupied with the fact that I was stuck in a hotel in Grand Rapids, MI, with no food. And, further, not one of those men on that team had even considered that I might be stranded over there, because not one of them had called to check on me.

I was about to give way to my frustrations and do a little men-bashing (and their illogical thought process) in my mind when I remembered who and Whose I am! I jumped up and said, "You know what, God? This is not my problem! This is YOUR problem! So I guess You have a plan, right? Okay, sure You do. Why am I stressing?"

It was about 8:30 P.M. by now, and I decided that surely I was hallucinating, because as soon as I started the dialogue with God, I could smell onions. Now, I really like onions, but I do not generally go around smelling them. But I knew I was not hallucinating; I could smell onions! I got dressed and made my way to the lobby. The smell of onions was stronger the closer I got. I asked that really tired clerk why she thought I might be smelling onions. She said it was probably that big six-foot-long hoagie that had been in the breakfast area. I peeked in there, and, sure enough, on the counter in the kitchen area, there was about two feet left of what had obviously been a longer sandwich. It was still wrapped and obviously untouched. She explained that there was a men's civic group staying at the hotel and they'd had a meeting in that area. They had called around town until they'd found someone to deliver in those risky weather conditions. They had much more food than they could eat and had never even unwrapped the end of the sandwich. They told her she could have it if she wanted so that it would not be wasted, but she did not like onions. If no one ate it, she guessed she would have to throw it out because it would need to be refrigerated overnight. DO YOU BELIEVE THAT??

I stood there, just shaking my head. It was more than enough for me! I asked if I could eat some of it and she insisted, provided that I could stand the smell of the onions. I chuckled. I cut the unwrapped sandwich (fresh and waiting for me), taking enough for right then and enough for the next day. I used the plastic wrap to wrap pieces individually. I went and asked her for an extra ice bucket, got some more tea, and returned to my room laughing. I filled my two ice buckets half-full with ice, laid my sandwiches on the ice, and closed the lid. Now I had refrigeration. I sat back and ate one of the best hoagies I had ever eaten, sipped me some tea, and marveled at my God. The next morning someone had come to open the breakfast bar, so I had my fruit and juice, got a few pastries, and went back to my room. At lunchtime, I took

73

my sandwich from my home-made refrigerator and enjoyed my lunch, including dessert. The "lake effect" had stopped and Grand Rapids began to come alive again, and one of my colleagues called to invite me to dinner with his family. I started to say something ugly, but I graciously accepted the invitation, knowing how my God provides and that I had BETTER NOT mess up my witness.

Of course, I shared my story and watched people marvel at the faithfulness of God. Even I marveled at the faithfulness of God. I had no idea what He would do, I just knew His track record and that He would do SOMETHING. I am fully persuaded that if I had not remembered that HE is my source, I NEVER would have smelled those onions, because what I did not tell you earlier is that my room was on the extreme end from the lobby and around a corner. There is no logical way that I should have been able to smell *anything* that was in the lobby.

BUT GOD IS AWESOME!

CHAPTER XXV

Who Would Have Ever Thought. . .

"For the Lord God is a sun and shield: the Lord will give grace and glory: no good thing will he withhold from them that walk uprightly."

Psalm 84:11 (KJV)

Last year, I had the awesome privilege of making the journey to Israel for the first time. I went with Aglow International, a worldwide Christian women's organization of which I have been a part for more than 25 years. When I knew in my heart that it was my year to go, I unwaveringly said to The Lord that I knew He was about to get me there even though it was way out of my budget. It was not long after I recognized the strong desire to go that I learned that if five people in a group paid to go, a sixth person would be named the group leader and go for the cost of the initial registration. That sounded really great, but why would anyone who had to pay over $2000 help me go for less than $350? Most of the groups I heard about split the cost between them once they got six people together, reducing everyone's cost by at least $500. I told The Lord that if I was to go, it was obviously HIS problem, so He could let me know when He worked it out.

It was not more than an hour later when a friend of mine came to me and said, "We are going to Israel."

I jokingly said, "Oh, so you're French now, with all this WE stuff."

She said, "Call me whatever you want, but The Lord says WE'RE going to Israel."

I said, "Okay, tell me more."

She began to tell me how three of them had decided that they were going to help me go to Israel, and it was up to me to find the two other people to complete the group. I began to get excited. God had placed the idea in someone else's heart to get ME to Israel!

Thinking it really was up to me, I started making some calls. I found another person who was willing to pay her full fare and name me as the group leader. I simply could not believe that people would do this. I heard of one more person who might be going, so I called her and asked her about being in our group. She said she would think about it.

A few weeks later, she called me back and declared that she indeed would not help me go for FREE if *she* had to pay to go. After all, I had a job. My feelings were a little hurt, but I got over it and went back to The Father. He simply said what I hate to hear when I am trying to figure something out, *"Trust me."*

I left things alone for a good while but was mentioning the trip all around just in case someone I was talking to was my sixth person. I got nowhere, and the deadline was fast approaching. I was sitting in my Monday night Bible study a few weeks later, and one of my students (my fifth person) very matter-of-factly said, "Oh, I have a sixth person for our trip to Israel. She is someone from my job who has finally gotten permission to go on this trip."

I sat there, looking at her like she had spoken some foreign language. I could not believe what I was hearing. God had prepared a person to go that I did not even know. He made sure that I knew He had done this and not me.

Needless to say, we all went to Israel! Of course, I hope you know that the adventure had only just begun. We were assigned to a bus and a tour guide for the entire trip. After a few days, your bus group became like your family. Each bus also had a captain. Each bus ate meals together and went on all the tours together. In addition, each group and its leader was kept together, so the six of us were together the entire ten days. We were a rowdy bunch and made the trip enjoyable. I love to sing, so I was constantly starting praise songs on the bus and keeping something fun going on. We traveled to many wonderful places, including Jerusalem, Capernaum, the Sea of Galilee, the Upper Room, Mount Carmel, and the Mount of Olives. We were in the Upper Room, and our bus captain came to me and asked if I would sing "The Lord's Prayer".

I looked at her as if she was not in her right mind and responded, "Me? Here?" She nodded and moved me to the center of the room. I nervously opened my mouth and began to sing "The Lord's Prayer", a capella. The sound bellowed from my innermost parts and I wondered who was singing. The acoustics were incredible and something supernatural was carrying my voice. I remember thinking that no one back home in Surry County, VA, or even Washington D.C., for that matter, was going to believe that I was in Israel, singing a solo in the middle of the Upper Room. I did not believe it myself!

As I approached the end of the song, something shifted, and it sounded like someone had started singing with me. The voices were too high to be the folks in that room with me. Somehow, I knew that angels were singing in that room. I know it sounds a bit much, but I know what I know!

Once we concluded our tour of the Upper Room and began to file out, heading back to the bus, I simply HAD to ask someone else what they'd heard. People said it sounded like angels were singing! That did it for me. I knew I was not hearing things. I wept in the presence of The Lord, totally humbled by His choice of me, knowing all that He knows about me. I felt like David in Psalm 139, when he said, "It is too high; I cannot attain unto it." I kept thinking that this experience was way up there in the "out of my league" category.

There were many more exciting experiences during that wonderful trip, and I guess you will just have to come and sit with me sometime to hear it all, but for right now, I simply want you to be as awed by God as I am that He would take such a simple earthen-clay vessel and perform mighty exploits, just to bring Himself glory. I am honored; I am humbled; I am amazed; I am yet expectant. I wait to see what my GOD will do in our encounters tomorrow and the many "everyday" days ahead.

About the Author

PAULETTE HOLLOWAY

Paulette Holloway acknowledges that God has always had a call upon her life and has only kept her because of HIS infinite mercy. She believes that God has saved her from a life of sin, abuse and confusion, for such a time as this.

Paulette hails from rural Virginia but has spent the past 29 years living in Washington, DC. She jokingly says she has raised seven children and survived, and has five beautiful grandchildren. She describes herself as a tenacious, high-energy, optimistic woman of integrity, who loves the word of God and loves life.

Paulette is a gifted teacher, speaker, evangelist, and missionary, who operates under the power of the Holy Spirit, using the Word of God as her mainstay. She loves people and speaks truth into the lives of those who let her. As an evangelist and missionary, she has traveled around the world spanning five continents serving God's people.

She currently serves on the area board of the Northern Virginia/ Washington, DC Aglow International, and served as the Monday night Aglow Bible study teacher for over thirteen years. She is an active member of All Nations Baptist Church in Washington, DC, where the Rev. Dr. James Coleman is her pastor.

Paulette holds a Bachelor's and a Masters of Social Work degree and is currently the Director of Bethany Christian Services, a Christian adoption agency in Maryland. She has completed her first book "Tea With God", highlighting a few of the encounters she has had with God over the years. She lifts up Proverbs 19:21 as her scripture of confidence, "Many are the plans in a man's heart, but it is the Lord's purpose that prevails (shall stand)", believing that even SHE cannot thwart the plans and purposes God has for her life. She desires daily to live to advance the kingdom of God as she joyfully walks toward her purpose.

ORDER FORM

Name _____

Company _____

Address _____

City _____ State _____ Zip _____

Telephone _____

Email _____

Please send me _____ copies of Tea With God.

Price	Shipping	Total
$10.00	$4.50 per book	$14.50

Total Enclosed: $_____

Books are available at special discounts for bulk purchases, sales promotions, fundraising, or educational purposes.

For more information about the author or speaking engagements, write to:

Paulette Holloway Ministries,
2017 North Capitol Street, NE
Washington, DC 20002

hollowayp@aol.com

Or order online at: www.wpublishers.com

1-888-925-BOOK (2665)